The
Social Work
Ethics
Casebook

Cases and Commentary

Frederic G. Reamer

NASW PRESS

National Association of Social Workers
Washington, DC

James J. Kelly, PhD, ACSW, LCSW, President
Elizabeth J. Clark, PhD, ACSW, MPH, Executive Director

Cheryl Y. Bradley, *Publisher*
Sarah Lowman, *Senior Editor*
Crystal McDonald, *Marketing Manager*
Juanita Ruffin, *Proofreader*
Bernice Eisen, *Indexer*

Cover design by Debra Naylor, Naylor Design, Inc., Washington DC
Interior design by Cynthia Stock, Electronic Quill, Silver Spring, MD
Printed by Victor Graphics, Baltimore, MD

Library of Congress Cataloging-in-Publication Data

Reamer, Frederic G., 1953–
    The social work ethics casebook : cases and commentary / Frederic G. Reamer.
        p.   cm.
    Includes bibliographical references and index.
    ISBN 978-0-87101-383-5
    1. Social service—Moral and ethical aspects—United States—Case studies.
2. Social workers—Professional ethics—Case studies. I. Title.
    HV41.R423 2009
    174ʹ.93613—dc22

                                                        2008039612

Printed in the United States of America

For
Deborah,
Emma,
and Leah

Contents

chapter one

The Nature of
Social Work Ethics

Social work ethics has come of age. From its modest beginnings in the late 19th century when social work was formally inaugurated as a profession, social work ethics has matured into one of the most critically important domains in social work practice, education, and professional development. Social work's earliest practitioners began their work in the profession without a code of ethics or professional literature on the subject. In fact, the first *National Association of Social Workers* (NASW) *Code of Ethics* was not ratified until 1960, more than a half century after social work's formal start.

Until the late 1970s, social work's ethics literature focused primarily on the profession's core values and several key issues related to client confidentiality, social workers' relationships with clients, and clients' right to self-determination. Following the emergence of bioethics as a discrete intellectual field in the mid-1970s and the simultaneous emergence of the broader discipline of professional ethics (sometimes known as practical ethics), in the early 1980s a small group of social work scholars and practitioners began exploring ethical issues in social work in much greater depth. Now the subject is taught much more deliberately in social work education programs and in continuing education conferences and courses sponsored by licensing boards and professional organizations. Also, social work and human services agencies—such as family service agencies, community mental health centers, schools, hospitals, home health care agencies, correctional facilities, substance abuse treatment programs, elder services programs, and public child welfare agencies—have developed ambitious ethics-related staff development offerings.

It is not surprising that social work's ethics literature has burgeoned in recent years. The current social work ethics literature focuses primarily on the topics of ethical dilemmas, ethical decision making (including frameworks and protocols), ethical theory, codes of ethics, ethics risk management (prevention of ethics complaints and lawsuits), and narrower topics such as boundary issues, dual relationships, conflicts of interest, informed consent, confidentiality and privileged communication, professional paternalism, ethics committees, ethics consultation, organizational ethics, ethics and managed care, and impaired practitioners.

Over time, social workers concerned about ethics education have discovered that case studies are compelling and essential. Social workers live their professional lives wrestling with complex case-related challenges. When is it appropriate to violate a client's right to confidentiality to protect a third party from harm? Under what circumstances is it ethical to interfere with a client's right to self-determination to protect the client from self-harm? What is the ethical way to resolve a potential conflict of interest when a qualified former client applies for a job at the social worker's agency and may become a colleague? How should a social worker act when she or he discovers that a valued colleague has behaved unethically? Is it ever permissible to deceive clients, even if it is "for their own good"? How should a social work administrator allocate limited agency resources when budget cuts impair her or his ability to meet clients' needs?

Case material brings ethics theories and concepts to life. Clearly, theories and concepts are important. They provide the conceptual guidance that professionals need to frame their assessments, program planning, interventions, and evaluations. But, theories and concepts by themselves can be sterile when presented in a vacuum. Wrapping theories and concepts around actual case material enriches social workers' understanding and insights. Cases provide a valuable lens through which to view and apply important theories and concepts.

This book includes a broad cross-section of ethics cases related to every core aspect of social work: clinical practice with individuals, families, couples, and small groups; community practice; policy practice; social justice and advocacy; administration and management; and research and evaluation. To fully appreciate the implications and relevance of ethics cases, it is important to understand the ways in which ethical standards and conceptual frameworks in social work have evolved. Much contemporary thinking on social work ethics resembles earlier perspectives; however, as we shall see, on other issues social workers' ethics-related perspectives have changed significantly over time. This shifting context provides a useful backdrop to the cases presented in this book.

The Evolution of Social Work Ethics

Social work's concern with ethics spans four major, sometimes overlapping, periods: the morality period, the values period, the ethical theory and decision-making period, and the ethical standards and risk management period.

THE MORALITY PERIOD. In the late 19th century, when social work was formally inaugurated as a profession, there was much more concern about the morality of the client than about the morality or ethics of the profession or its practitioners. Social workers' earliest practitioners focused on organized relief for people living in poverty and other vulnerable circumstances. Often this preoccupation took the form of paternalistic efforts to bolster poor people's morality and the rectitude of those who had succumbed to "shiftless" or "wayward" habits.

Social workers' focus on the morality of poor people waned significantly during the settlement house movement in the early 20th century, when many social workers turned their attention to structural and environmental causes of individual and social problems, particularly social workers' ethical obligation to promote social justice and social reform. As has been well documented in the profession's literature, many social workers were concerned with "cause" rather than, or in addition to, "case." This was evident in social workers' social reform efforts designed to address the toxic environmental determinants of problems related to poverty, inadequate housing and health care, mental illness, alcoholism, and violence.

Emphasis on clients' morality continued to weaken during the next several decades as social workers created and refined various intervention theories and strategies, training programs, and educational models. During this phase, many social workers were more concerned about cultivating perspectives and methods that would be indigenous to social work, partly in an effort to distinguish social work's approach to helping from those of allied professions, such as psychology and psychiatry.

THE VALUES PERIOD. Although a critical mass of serious scholarship on social work ethics did not appear until the 1950s, there were several efforts earlier in the 20th century to explore social work values and ethics. As early as 1919 there were attempts to draft professional codes of ethics. In 1922 the Family Welfare Association of America appointed an ethics committee in response to questions about ethical problems in social work. In addition, there is evidence that at least some schools of social work were teaching discrete courses on values and ethics in the 1920s.

By the late 1940s and early 1950s, social workers' concern about the moral dimensions of the profession shifted. Instead of the earlier preoccupation with clients' morality, social workers began to focus much more on the morality, values, and ethics of the profession and its practitioners. Nearly a half century after its formal beginning, social work began to develop and publicize ethical standards and guidelines. In 1947, after several years of discussion and debate, the Delegate Conference of the American Association of Social Workers adopted a code of ethics. Several social work journals also published several seminal articles on values and ethics. In 1959 Muriel Pumphrey published her landmark work, *The Teaching of Values and Ethics in Social Work Education*, for the Council on Social Work Education.

In the 1960s and early 1970s, social workers directed considerable attention toward matters of social justice, social reform, and civil rights. The social turbulence of this era had enormous influence on the profession. Thousands of new practitioners were attracted to the profession primarily because of social work's abiding concern about values germane to human rights, welfare rights, equality, discrimination, and oppression. It is significant that NASW adopted its first code of ethics during this period.

Particularly important during this period was the proliferation of commentary on core social work values. These discussions of social work values were of three types. One group included broad descriptive overviews of the profession's mission and its core values, such as respect of people, valuing individuals' capacity for change, client self-determination, client empowerment, individual worth and dignity, commitment to social change and social justice, service to others, professional competence, professional integrity, providing individuals with opportunity to realize their potential, seeking to meet individuals' common human needs, client privacy and confidentiality, nondiscrimination, equal opportunity, respect of diversity, and willingness to transmit professional knowledge and skills to others. A second group of discussions included critiques of social work values. Finally, a third group of discussions included reports of empirical research on values held or embraced by social workers.

During this period many social workers focused on the need for social workers to examine and clarify their own personal values. The premise here was that social workers' personal beliefs and values related, for example, to people living in poverty, race relations, abortion, homosexuality, civil disobedience, and drug use would have a profound effect on their approach to and relationships with clients.

THE ETHICAL THEORY AND DECISION-MAKING PERIOD. Social work entered a new phase in the early 1980s, influenced largely by the invention in the 1970s of a new field known as applied and professional ethics (sometimes known as practical ethics). The principal feature of the applied and professional ethics field, which began especially with developments in medical ethics, or what has become known as bioethics, was the deliberate, disciplined attempt to apply principles, concepts, and theories of moral philosophy, or ethics, to real-life challenges faced by professionals. For decades prior to this development, moral philosophers had been preoccupied with fairly abstract debates about the meaning of ethical terms and the validity of rather abstruse ethical theories and conceptually complex moral arguments, a philosophical specialty known as meta-ethics. Several factors, however, inspired a substantial contingent of moral philosophers to turn their attention to more practical and immediate ethical problems. First, intense social debate in the 1960s concerning such prominent issues as welfare rights, prisoners' rights, patients' rights, women's rights, human rights, and affirmative action led many moral philosophers to grapple with contemporary issues. Second, a number of technological developments, particularly related to health care issues (for example, reproduction, organ transplantation, abortion, and end-of-life decisions), led many moral philosophers to explore applied ethical issues. In addition, increasingly widespread media publicity related to moral scandals and ethical misconduct in public and professional life, beginning especially with Watergate in the early 1970s, stirred up interest in professional ethics. It was during this period that now-prominent ethics organizations got their formal start, most notably the Hastings Center and the Kennedy Institute of Ethics at Georgetown University. (The number of applied and professional ethics organizations has grown so large that there is now a national Association for Practical and Professional Ethics.)

Along with most other professions—including nursing, medicine, journalism, engineering, dentistry, law, psychology, counseling, and business—social work's literature on ethics began to change significantly in the early 1980s. In addition to discussions about the profession's values, a small group of scholars began to write about ethical issues and challenges while drawing on literature, concepts, theories, and principles from the traditional field of moral philosophy and the newer field of applied and professional ethics. Using somewhat different approaches, several social workers acknowledged explicitly for the first time the relevance of moral philosophy and ethical theory, concepts, and principles in the analysis and resolution of ethical issues in social work. Furthermore, the 1987 edition of the NASW *Encyclopedia of Social Work* included an article directly addressing the relevance of philosophical and ethical concepts to social work ethics.

Since the early and mid-1980s, literature on social work ethics that draws directly on ethical theory and concepts has burgeoned. Most of this literature explores the relationship between standard ethical theories (known as deontology, teleology, consequentialism, utilitarianism, and virtue theory) and actual or hypothetical ethical dilemmas encountered by social workers. Relevant ethical dilemmas concern direct practice and clinical practice (for example, confidentiality, client self-determination, informed consent, professional paternalism, truth telling, conflicts of interest), program design and agency administration (for example, adhering to agency policies or regulations and distributing limited resources), and relationships among practitioners (for example, reporting colleagues' unethical behavior or impairment). Examples include social workers who must decide between their duty to respect the client's rights to confidentiality and their obligation to protect third parties from harm; whether to place limits on the client's right to engage in self-destructive behavior; how to allocate scarce or limited resources; whether to comply with an allegedly unjust law or regulation; and whether to "blow the whistle" and report a professional colleague's ethical misconduct to authorities.

A significant portion of the literature since the mid-1980s has focused on decision-making strategies social workers can engage in when faced with difficult ethical judgments. Typically, these discussions identify a series of steps and considerations social workers can follow as they attempt to resolve difficult ethical dilemmas, focusing on the conflicting values, ethical duties, and obligations; the individuals, groups, and organizations that are likely to be affected; possible courses of action; relevant ethical theories, principles, and guidelines; legal principles and pertinent codes of ethics; social work practice theory and principles; personal values; the need to consult with colleagues and appropriate experts; and the need to monitor, evaluate, and document decisions.

ETHICAL STANDARDS AND RISK MANAGEMENT PERIOD. The most recent stage reflects the remarkable growth in social workers' understanding of ethical issues in the profession. It is marked primarily by the 1996 ratification of the NASW *Code of Ethics*, which significantly expanded ethical guidelines and standards for social work practice.

As I noted earlier, few formal ethical standards existed early in social work's history. The earliest known attempt to formulate a code was an experimental draft code of ethics attributed to Mary Richmond. Although several other social work organizations developed draft codes during social work's early years (for example, the American Association for Organizing Family Social Work and several chapters of the American Association of Social Workers), it was not until 1947 that the latter group adopted a formal code. In 1960 NASW adopted its first code of ethics, five years after the association was formed.

Codes of Ethics

The 1960 NASW *Code of Ethics* consisted of only 14 proclamations concerning, for example, every social worker's duty to give precedence to professional responsibility over personal interests; to respect the privacy of clients; to give appropriate professional service in public emergencies; and to contribute knowledge, skills, and support to human welfare programs. A series of brief first-person statements (such as, "I give precedence to my professional responsibility over my personal interests," and, "I respect the privacy of the people I serve," [p. 1]) were preceded by a preamble that set forth social workers' responsibilities to uphold humanitarian ideals, maintain and improve social work service, and develop the philosophy and skills of the profession. In 1967 a 15th principle pledging nondiscrimination was added to the proclamations.

In 1977, based in part on growing concern about this code's level of abstraction and usefulness, NASW established a task force chaired by Charles Levy to revise the code. In 1979 NASW adopted a new code, which was far more ambitious than the 1960 code. The 1979 code included nearly 80 ethical "principles" divided into six major sections of brief, unannotated statements with a preamble describing the code's general purpose and stating that the code's principles provided guidelines for the enforcement of ethical practices in the profession. The code included major sections concerning social workers' general conduct and comportment and ethical responsibilities to clients, colleagues, employers, employing organizations, the social work profession, and society.

The 1979 code was revised twice (NASW, 1990, 1993) as a result of several important developments. In 1990 several principles related to solicitation of clients and fee splitting were modified following an inquiry, begun in 1986, into NASW policies by the U.S. Federal Trade Commission (FTC). The FTC alleged that the code's prohibition of client solicitation and fee splitting constituted an inappropriate restraint of trade. As a result of the inquiry, principles in the code were revised to remove prohibitions concerning solicitation of clients from colleagues or one's agency and to modify wording related to accepting compensation for making a referral.

In 1992 an NASW task force, which I chaired, recommended that five specific new principles addressing two new concepts be added to the code. Three of the principles concerned the problem of social worker impairment, and two concerned the problem of dual or multiple relationships between social workers and clients. Both the problem of social worker impairment and dual and multiple relationships between social workers and clients had begun to receive increasing attention in the profession and, the task force argued, needed to be acknowledged in the code. In 1993 the NASW Delegate Assembly voted to add these five new principles.

By the time of the 1993 NASW Delegate Assembly, there was growing awareness among social workers that the NASW *Code of Ethics* required significant revision and that modest changes and "tinkering" would no longer suffice. The vast majority of the scholarly literature on social work ethics had been published since the ratification of the 1979 code, which went into effect as the broader field of applied and professional ethics was in its infancy. There was widespread recognition that issues explored in social work, not to mention the broader applied and professional ethics field, since the ratification of the 1979 code needed to be reflected in a new code. Examples included new knowledge and discussions related to ethical misconduct, ethical decision making, informed consent, dual and multiple relationships and related boundary issues, confidentiality and the protection of third parties, privileged communication, electronic communications, ethical issues in social work supervision, ethics consultation, ethical issues in industrial social work, the teaching of social work ethics, ethics and unionization, ethical issues in organizations, impaired social workers, ethics in social work research and evaluation, professional paternalism, bioethical issues in social work, ethics committees, professional malpractice, and social work's moral mission.

Because of the exponential growth of ethics-related knowledge—with respect to social work in particular and the professions in general—since the development of the 1979 code, delegates at the 1993 NASW Delegate Assembly recognized the need for an entirely new code. In addition, there was widespread recognition that the profession's code needed to pay more attention to ethical issues facing social workers not involved in direct practice and clinical practice, especially social workers involved in agency administration, supervision, research and evaluation, and education. Thus, the Delegate Assembly passed a resolution to establish a task force to draft a completely new code of ethics for submission to the 1996 Delegate Assembly. The task force was established to produce a new code that would be far more comprehensive and relevant to current practice, taking into consideration the tremendous increase in knowledge since the ratification of the 1979 code.

The Code of Ethics Revision Committee was appointed in 1994 by the president of NASW and spent two years drafting a new code designed to incorporate comprehensive guidelines reflecting the impressive expansion of knowledge in the field. The committee, which I chaired, included a moral philosopher active in the professional ethics field and social workers from a variety of practice and academic settings.[1] During the two-year period leading up to the final draft of the new code, the committee reviewed literature on social work ethics and on applied and professional

---

1. Members of the committee included Carol Brill, Jacqueline Glover, Marjorie Hammock, M. Vincentia Joseph, Alfred Murillo, Jr., Frederic Reamer [chair], Barbara Varley, and Drayton Vincent.

ethics generally to identify key concepts and issues that might be addressed in the new code, reviewed the 1979 code (as revised) to identify content that should be retained or deleted and areas where content might be added, issued formal invitations to all NASW members and to members of various social work organizations (the National Association of Black Social Workers, the Council on Social Work Education, the American Association of State Social Work Boards, and the National Federation of Societies of Clinical Social Work) to suggest issues that might be addressed in the new code, shared rough drafts of the code with a small group of ethics experts in social work and other professions for their comments, and revised the code on the basis of the various sources of feedback. The draft code was published in the *NASW News*, along with an invitation for all NASW members to submit comments to be considered by the committee as it prepared the final draft for submission to the 1996 Delegate Assembly. Committee members also met with each of the NASW Delegate Assembly regional coalitions to discuss the code's development and content and to receive delegates' comments and feedback. The code was then presented to and overwhelmingly ratified by the Delegate Assembly.

The current code, which is clearly the most comprehensive set of ethical standards in social work, reflects the state of the art in social work ethics (see Appendix). The code's preamble signifies a remarkable event in social work's history. For the first time in NASW's history, the code of ethics includes a formally sanctioned mission statement and an explicit summary of the profession's core values. The Code of Ethics Revision Committee felt strongly that the profession's code should include a forceful statement of social work's moral aims, drawing on the profession's time-honored commitments and contemporary concerns. The mission statement emphasizes social work's historic and enduring commitment to enhancing well-being and helping meet the basic needs of all people (Towle, 1965), with particular attention to the needs and empowerment of people who are vulnerable, oppressed, and living in poverty. The mission statement stresses social work's venerated concern about vulnerable populations and the profession's traditional simultaneous focus on individual well-being and the environmental forces that create, contribute to, and address problems in living. The preamble also emphasizes social workers' determination to promote social justice and social change with and on behalf of clients.

A particularly noteworthy feature of the preamble is the inclusion of six core values on which social work's mission is based: service, social justice, dignity and worth of the person, importance of human relationships, integrity, and competence. The Code of Ethics Revision Committee settled on these core values after engaging in a systematic and comprehensive review of literature on the subject.

9

The code also provides a brief guide for dealing with ethical issues or dilemmas in social work practice. Drawing on literature on ethical decision making in social work, this section highlights various resources social workers should consider when they encounter challenging ethical decisions, including ethical theory, literature on ethical decision-making strategies, social work practice theory and research, relevant laws and regulations, agency policies, and other relevant codes of ethics. Social workers are also encouraged to obtain ethics consultation when appropriate, perhaps from an agency-based or social work organization's ethics committee, regulatory bodies (for example, a state licensing board), knowledgeable colleagues, supervisors, or legal counsel.

The code's most extensive section, "Ethical Standards," greatly expands the number of specific ethical guidelines contained in the code, again reflecting increased knowledge in the profession. The 155 specific ethical standards are designed to guide social workers' conduct, reduce malpractice and liability risks, and provide a basis for adjudication of ethics complaints filed against NASW members (the standards are also used by other bodies that have chosen to adopt the code, such as state licensing and regulatory boards, professional liability insurance providers, courts of law, agency boards of directors, and government agencies). In general, the code's standards concern three kinds of issues: (1) what are usually considered to be "mistakes" social workers might make that have ethical implications (for example, mentioning clients' names in public or semipublic areas, forgetting to renew a client's expired release of information form before disclosing sensitive documents to a third party, or overlooking an important agency policy concerning termination of services), (2) difficult ethical decisions faced by social workers that have reasonable arguments for and against different courses of action (for example, decisions about whether to disclose confidential information to protect a third party, how to allocate scarce or limited agency resources, whether to honor a picket line at one's employment setting, whether to obey an unjust law or regulation, or whether to interfere with a client who willingly is engaging in self-destructive behavior), and (3) ethical misconduct (for example, sexual exploitation of clients, conflicts of interest, deliberate misrepresentation, or fraudulent activity).

The code's standards fall into six substantive categories concerning social workers' ethical responsibilities to clients, to colleagues, in practice settings, as professionals, to the profession, and to society at large. The first section, Ethical Responsibilities to Clients, is the most detailed and comprehensive because it addresses a wide range of issues involved in the delivery of services to individuals, families, couples, and small groups of clients. In addition to more detailed standards on topics also addressed in the 1979 code (for example, client self-determination, privacy and confidentiality, client access to records, sexual relationships with clients, payment for services, termination of services), the code addresses a number of new issues: the provision of services by electronic media (such as computers, telephone, radio, and television); social workers' competence in the areas of cultural and social diversity; use of intervention approaches for which recognized standards do not exist; dual and multiple relationships with former clients, colleagues, and students; confidentiality issues involving families, couples, and group counseling, contact with media representatives, electronic records and electronic communications (such as the use of electronic mail and facsimile machines), consultation, and deceased clients; sexual relationships with former clients or clients' relatives or friends; physical contact with clients; sexual harassment; derogatory language; and bartering for services.

The section in the code on ethical responsibilities to colleagues includes newer content on issues related to interdisciplinary collaboration; consultation with colleagues; referral of clients for services; sexual relationships with supervisees, trainees, or other colleagues over whom social workers exercise professional authority; sexual harassment of supervisees, students, trainees, or colleagues; and unethical conduct of colleagues. The section on ethical responsibilities in practice settings addresses new issues related to supervision and consultation; education and training; documentation in case records; billing practices; client transfer; administration; continuing education and staff development; challenging unethical practices in employment settings; and labor–management disputes. The section on ethical responsibilities as professionals addresses new issues related to social workers' competence; misrepresentation of qualifications, credentials, education, areas of expertise, affiliations, services provided, and results to be achieved; and solicitation of clients. The section on ethical responsibilities to the social work profession addresses new issues related to dissemination of knowledge, especially evaluation and research. This section includes a greatly expanded set of standards concerning social workers' obligation to evaluate policies, programs, and practice interventions; use evaluation and research evidence in their professional practice; follow guidelines to protect individuals who participate in evaluation and research; and accurately disseminate results. The final section—Ethical Responsibilities to the Broader Society—addresses new issues related to social workers' involvement in social and political action. The code includes more explicit and forceful language concerning social workers' obligation to address social justice issues, particularly pertaining to vulnerable, disadvantaged, oppressed, and exploited people and groups.

Changes in social workers' understanding of and approach to ethical issues represent one of the most significant developments in the profession's century-long history. What began as fairly modest and superficial concern about moral issues in the late 19th and early 20th centuries has evolved into an ambitious attempt to grasp and resolve complex ethical challenges. Social workers' early preoccupation with their clients' morality is now overshadowed by social workers' efforts to identify and dissect ethical dilemmas, apply thoughtful decision-making tools, manage ethics-related risks that could lead to litigation, and confront ethical misconduct in the profession.

We explore these diverse issues in the case studies that follow. The cases in this book are based on actual circumstances. Identifying information has been changed to protect individuals' privacy and confidentiality. The commentary that follows each case provides points of departure for discussion and constructive debate. Each commentary includes a summary of key ethical issues and citations of relevant standards in the NASW *Code of Ethics*. Each section concludes with several discussion questions.

The relatively brief case studies and discussions cannot possibly capture all of the complexity and subtleties that typically emerge when all relevant facts are known. Readers are encouraged to develop their own commentaries and analyses on the basis of their unique interpretation of the case-related facts and relevant social work concepts and standards.

References

Towle, C. (1965). *Common human needs*. Washington, DC: National Association of Social Workers.

National Association of Social Workers. (1990). *Code of ethics of the National Association of Social Workers*. Washington, DC: Author.

National Association of Social Workers. (1993). *Code of ethics of the National Association of Social Workers*. Washington, DC: Author.

chapter two

Ethical Responsibilities to Clients

Social workers encounter various ethical issues in their work with individual clients, couples, families, and small groups. Common issues involve social workers' commitment to clients; client self-determination; informed consent; social workers' competence to work with clients; cultural competence and social diversity; conflicts of interest and boundaries; privacy and confidentiality; client access to records; sexual relationships between social workers and current and former clients; sexual relationships between social workers and clients' relatives or other individuals with whom social workers maintain a close personal relationship; physical contact with clients; sexual harassment of clients; social workers' use of derogatory language; client payment for services; serving clients who lack decision-making capacity; interruption of services; and termination of services.

Commitment to Clients

CASE 2.1. A clinical social worker at a family service agency provided counseling services to individuals and families. The agency had a contract with the local school district to provide clinical services to students who are referred by school personnel. The school district typically refers students to the family service agency when its student assistance counselors conclude that a student requires intensive, relatively long-term counseling.

The social worker received a referral involving a nine-year-old boy. According to the student assistance counselor at the boy's school, the boy's teacher has been concerned for some time about the boy's classroom behavior and academic performance. According to the teacher, the boy is difficult to control; he is often disruptive in class, treats other children aggressively, and is impulsive. The teacher also reported that the boy is struggling academically and is having difficulty completing school-based tasks in a timely manner. The boy also manifests some symptoms of depression.

The social worker arranged to meet with the boy and his mother, a single parent. After conducting a thorough biopsychosocial assessment, the social worker began meeting with the boy weekly. In addition, the social worker collaborated with the boy's teacher to develop a behavior management strategy for the teacher to use in the classroom (on the basis of commonly used behavioral principles). The social worker also referred the boy to a local psychiatrist for possible psychotropic medication. After about six weeks both the boy's teacher and the boy's mother reported considerable improvement in the boy's behavior and academic performance.

After the third week of intervention, the boy's mother called the social worker and asked for an appointment to discuss issues with which she is struggling, including her ongoing substance abuse. The two met and the mother explained that she would like to meet with the social worker for a number of sessions to talk about her own problems, particularly as they affect her son. The mother and social worker met weekly for two and one-half months. Most of their discussions focused on the mother's distress about the deterioration of her marriage to the boy's father, her substance abuse issues, and her own symptoms of depression.

At the beginning of their 10th meeting, the mother told the social worker that she needed to tell her something important. The mother explained that she has been harboring a secret. The mother then told the social worker that she has been living under an assumed name because she fears that her husband, from whom she is seeking a divorce, might find her and continue to abuse her emotionally. The mother disclosed her real name to the social worker and explained that her husband has been quite abusive—emotionally, not physically. The mother told the social worker that months earlier she had warned her husband that if he continued to abuse her emotionally, "he was going to get up one morning and find that his son and I had left for good."

The mother reported that her husband told his divorce lawyer about his wife's threat, and the lawyer had obtained a court order prohibiting the mother from leaving the court's jurisdiction without permission while the divorce and custody dispute were pending. Despite the court order, however, the mother left with her son in the middle of the night following a heated encounter with her husband. The mother traveled with her son across two state lines and settled in her current community, where a close friend of hers lives. The mother began living under the assumed name to hide from her husband. She enrolled her son in the local school where he had been having difficulty.

The mother told the social worker, "I just had to tell you about this part of my life. You've really been helpful to me and I've felt so guilty about keeping this secret from you. I assume you won't tell anybody what I've just told you."

Discussion

Social workers have always recognized that their primary responsibility is to their clients. However, on occasion, instances arise when social workers find themselves caught between their clients' and the broader society's interests. As the NASW *Code of Ethics* states,

> Social workers' primary responsibility is to promote the well-being of clients. In general, clients' interests are primary. However, social workers' responsibility to the larger society or specific legal obligations may on limited occasions supersede the loyalty owed clients, and clients should be so advised. (Examples include when a social worker is required by law to report that a client has abused a child or has threatened to harm self or others.) (standard 1.01)

In this case, the social worker encountered diverse conflicts. Her client was actively violating the law, in that she transported her child across state lines despite a court order prohibiting her from leaving the court's jurisdiction while her divorce and custody dispute were pending. Thus the social worker had to decide whether her commitment to her client took precedence over her duty to "the larger society or specific legal obligations" associated with the court order and the mother's apparent violation of the law.

In addition, the social worker encountered a conflict of interest involving the mother and son. Initially the social worker provided services to the son. Subsequently, the mother approached the social worker and requested services. As a result, the social worker became involved in a "dual relationship," in that she entered into a clinical relationship with two people who have a relationship with each other and whose interests might conflict. If (and this is a matter for debate) the social worker concluded that the mother's actions—taking the son away from his father, in violation of a court order, transporting him across state lines, living under an assumed name—endangered the child and constituted emotional abuse, the social worker would be obligated under state law to report the mother to child welfare authorities. One might argue that the social worker should have explained the potential conflict of interest to the mother and offered to help her find another practitioner who could assist her. According to the NASW *Code of Ethics*,

> When social workers provide services to two or more people who have a relationship with each other (for example, couples, family members), social

workers should clarify with all parties which individuals will be considered clients and the nature of social workers' professional obligations to the various individuals who are receiving services. Social workers who anticipate a conflict of interest among the individuals receiving services or who anticipate having to perform in potentially conflicting roles (for example, when a social worker is asked to testify in a child custody dispute or divorce proceedings involving clients) should clarify their role with the parties involved and take appropriate action to minimize any conflict of interest. (Standard 1.06[d])

In addition to considering the state mandatory reporting law concerning suspected child abuse and neglect, the social worker would also have to consider several other relevant laws. The most relevant laws include the following:

- Confidentiality of Alcohol and Drug Abuse Patient Records (42 C.F.R. §2-1 ff.): This regulation broadly protects the confidentiality of the records maintained in connection with any program or activity relating to substance abuse education, prevention, training, treatment, rehabilitation, or research that is conducted, regulated, or directly or indirectly funded by any federal department or agency. This regulation is relevant in this case because the mother spoke with the social worker about her substance abuse issues and the social worker's agency receives federal funds for some of its programs. Although the regulation strictly prohibits disclosures of confidential information, it includes exceptions. One of the permitted exceptions concerns disclosure of confidential information to child welfare authorities related to suspected child abuse or neglect.
- Health Insurance Portability and Accountability Act (HIPAA–Public Law 104-91): HIPAA requires that professional health-related information be kept confidential. As with the Confidentiality of Alcohol and Drug Abuse Patient Records regulations, HIPAA includes exceptions for disclosure of confidential information concerning child abuse.
- Uniform Child Custody Jurisdiction Act (UCCJA) of 1968
- Uniform Child Custody Jurisdiction and Enforcement Act (UCCJEA) of 1996
- Parental Kidnapping Prevention Act of 1981 (PKPA)

Ideally the social worker would use her clinical skills and therapeutic alliance with the mother to help her chart a constructive course of action that would lead the mother to take responsibility for her decisions, collaborate with local child welfare and law enforcement officials, and avoid disclosure by the social worker. If that strategy does not succeed, the social worker would need to consult with colleagues, review relevant ethical standards and laws, and make a decision about the conflict between her duty to her clients and her obligation to the broader society and its laws. To protect both the clients and the social worker, the practitioner should have discussed confidentiality and its limitations with her clients at the beginning of the relationship so that the clients fully understood the ramifications of disclosures they might make. According to the NASW *Code of Ethics*,

> Social workers should discuss with clients and other interested parties the nature of confidentiality and limitations of clients' right to confidentiality. Social workers should review with clients circumstances where confidential information may be requested and where disclosure of confidential information may be legally required. This discussion should occur as soon as possible in the social worker–client relationship and as needed throughout the course of the relationship. (standard 1.07[e])

The overarching issue here is that social workers sometimes have to make difficult judgments about whether their responsibility to the larger society supersedes their commitment to clients. Historically, social workers in the United States became especially aware of this conflict in the 1960s, when many state laws began to require disclosure of confidential information, sometimes against clients' wishes, concerning suspected child abuse and neglect. Although many social workers were initially concerned about the possible impact of these reporting requirements, particularly with respect to the possibility that they would erode clients' trust in social workers, in general the profession has come to accept that professional responsibility entails reconciling occasional conflicts between their clients' and others' interests (including, for example, when a client threatens to harm a spouse, partner, or acquaintance).

In some circumstances in which there is a possible conflict between clients' interests and the broader society's interests, social workers should give clients the benefit of the doubt. An example is when a client informs a social worker that five years earlier she or he sold drugs illegally. Although there might be some public benefit if the social worker were to disclose this information to the police (so the client could be prosecuted), current ethical norms concerning confidentiality (to be discussed later) and public policy suggest that, overall, such a disclosure would lead to more harm than good, particularly with respect to the public's willingness to trust social workers. Social workers generally agree that in such cases they should not place the broader society's immediate interests above clients' interests. One argument is that, in the long run, the broader society's interests are better served if people are willing to place their trust in social workers and share with them embarrassing or incriminating information about their lives that pertains to issues they wish to address in counseling.

In other circumstances, however, clients' interests are outweighed by the broader society's interests or by some legal requirement. A compelling example would be a parent who asks a social worker not to inform child welfare officials that he or she severely beat his or her newborn infant. In this instance, the social worker would have an obligation to protect the vulnerable child.

Sometimes it may not be clear whether the client's or the broader society's interests, or a legal requirement, should take precedence. Examples include when a client discloses information about a serious health condition that could impair the client's driving ability and asks the social worker not to share this information with anyone, and when a client who is a mental health counselor tells the social worker that he or she has been sexually involved with a client. In the latter instance, if the social worker discloses this information to authorities (for example, the state board that licenses the mental health counselor, who is also the social worker's client) the client may not get the therapeutic help he needs; at the same time, the social worker may be concerned that the client poses a threat to the public and that disclosure is necessary to prevent harm. In these instances, reasonable social workers may disagree about the nature of their ethical duties to clients and the broader public. In such circumstances social workers would be wise to carefully review relevant ethical standards, laws, regulations, and professional literature. Collegial consultation is essential.

NASW *CODE OF ETHICS* STANDARDS: Commitment to Clients (1.01); Self-Determination (1.02); Informed Consent (1.03); Conflicts of Interest (1.06); Privacy and Confidentiality (1.07); Consultation (2.05)

DISCUSSION QUESTIONS:
1. Social workers agree that their primary obligation is to their clients. However, in some circumstances social workers' obligation to the broader society may override clients' rights or interests. Describe three circumstances in which social workers' obligation to the broader society would override clients' rights or interests.
2. You are the clinical director in a community mental health center. The agency director has asked you to write a new policy summarizing the

circumstances under which the agency's obligation to the broader society would override clients' rights or interests. What key points would you include in this policy?

Self-Determination and Paternalism

CASE 2.2. A social worker in a suburban hospital worked with patients and their families. His primary duty was to provide information and support to patients and serve as a resource to family members.

The social worker received a phone call from the adult son of an elderly patient. The patient had signed a consent form authorizing the social worker to confer with her son. The son told the social worker that his mother's doctor just informed him that his mother's recent medical tests show that she has a very serious case of uterine cancer. The son pleaded with the social worker to not share with his mother the physician's dire prognosis, even if his mother asks for detailed information. According to the son, the patient struggles with serious clinical depression and cognitive impairment and would have a very difficult time processing this troubling information. On the basis of his contact with the patient, the social worker also was concerned about the patient's ability to cope with discouraging details about her health.

Three days later the social worker visited with the patient. During the conversation the patient said to the social worker, "I don't really know what's going on here. I feel like my body is breaking down, but no one is explaining to me what's happening. Have you heard anything about what's wrong with me and what the doctor plans to do?"

CASE 2.3. A social worker in a domestic violence shelter met with a woman who had been at the shelter for two days. The social worker interviewed the woman and learned that she has been in an abusive relationship for nearly four years. Several days earlier the woman and her husband argued, and the husband beat the woman with a broom handle. The woman had visible scars on her arm and a laceration on her face.

According to the woman, her husband has a serious drinking problem and, when he is drunk, sometimes physically abuses her. The woman told the social worker that she has stayed in other shelters five or six times.

The woman also told the social worker that she wants to give her husband "another chance." The woman said, "He's usually fine when he's not drinking. He's really not a bad man. He's told me how sorry he is and that it won't happen again."

The social worker had years of experience working with battered women. On the basis of her extensive experience, the social worker strongly believed that the woman is likely to be abused again if she returns to her husband, particularly because the man has not taken any steps to address his alcohol and domestic violence problems. The social worker knew that, on the one hand, she was obligated ethically to respect her client's right to self-determination. But the social worker also had a very strong feeling that she should try to convince the woman to not return to her husband given the history of his abusive behavior. The social worker was eager to protect the woman from the consequences of her own judgment.

Discussion

Most social workers are drawn to the profession because of their genuine desire to help people who are struggling with serious problems in living, such as poverty, homelessness, domestic violence, substance abuse, mental illness, physical disability, and so on. Social workers typically embrace the profession's deep-seated commitment to the principle of client self-determination, which ordinarily means that clients have the right to make their own choices and chart the course of their lives. As the NASW *Code of Ethics* states,

> Social workers respect and promote the right of clients to self-determination and assist clients in their efforts to identify and clarify their goals. Social workers may limit clients' right to self-determination when, in the social workers' professional judgment, clients' actions or potential actions pose a serious, foreseeable, and imminent risk to themselves or others. (standard 1.02)

Social workers have always emphasized the importance of clients' right to self-determination. However, social workers have paid less attention to their occasional inclination to interfere with clients' self-determination to protect clients "from themselves" and their own questionable judgment. Interfering with clients "for their own good" is known as professional paternalism.

Paternalism in social work can occur in three different ways. The first occurs when a social worker believes that it is justifiable to withhold information from clients for their own good. In these instances social workers conclude that sharing accurate, candid information with clients would harm them. This may include information about mental health diagnoses and prognoses, health, and so on. For example, a social worker may believe that if the client obtained accurate information about her very uncertain psychiatric prognosis, the client may "give up" and not invest herself in treatment. As a result, the social worker may decide to withhold information. Or, as in case 2.2, the social worker may be concerned about the client's emotional and cognitive wherewithal to process troubling information. One might call this passive paternalism, in that it entails failing to provide information, as opposed to actively giving clients false information.

A second form of paternalism involves lying to clients and deliberately giving them false information—what one might call active paternalism. In these instances, social workers believe that benevolent deception is in clients' best interest. Social workers who believe this form of paternalism is justifiable conclude that actively misleading clients is necessary to protect clients from their self-destructive tendencies. For example, a social worker would be actively paternalistic if he or she gave the client false information when the client asked about the likelihood that he or she would be released soon from a psychiatric hospital. The social worker might believe that active deception is justifiable if giving the client false hope—based on an overly optimistic report about the client's likely discharge—might prevent the client from attempting to commit suicide.

A third form of paternalism involves physically interfering with a client or attempting to influence a client in a way that the client resents or rejects. In case 2.3, for example, the social worker had to decide whether to honor the client's stated intention to return to her abusive husband or to try to talk the client out of her plan. Another example of this form of paternalism involves social workers who try to convince—or even force—a homeless person to go to a shelter for his or her own good because of the threat of subzero temperatures, even though the person is adamant that he or she does not want to go to the shelter.

The debate concerning paternalism and whether there are limits to social workers' and others' obligation to protect people from harm—whether by use of deception, persuasion, or coercion—has a long history. In social work the controversy is centered on the tension between practitioners who believe in clients' fundamental right to self-determination—the freedom to choose life goals, take risks, and make mistakes—and practitioners who believe that at least some degree of deception, persuasion, or coercion is justifiable, and may be necessary, to protect vulnerable clients from harm and injury.

The concept of paternalism has been controversial since Aristotle's time, although the term itself is a contemporary one. Modern debate about the nature and limits of paternalism was especially intense during the 1960s, fueled largely by the period's widespread focus on civil rights and civil liberties issues. Debate about paternalistic treatment of people who have mental and physical disabilities or who are poor, prisoners, and children stimulated a great deal of speculation and opinion about the limits of paternalistic deception, persuasion, and coercion. Typical examples of paternalism issues include laws, regulations, and rules that permit involuntary commitment of people to psychiatric facilities to prevent them from harming themselves; requiring members of certain religious groups to receive medical treatment to protect their health; outlawing suicide; prohibiting swimming when no lifeguard is on duty; and requiring motorcyclists to wear safety helmets.

Clearly, cases 2.2 and 2.3 raise important paternalism issues. In case 2.2 the hospital social worker had to decide whether to withhold information from his vulnerable client because of his and the patient's son's concern about her emotional and cognitive vulnerability. In case 2.3 the social worker in the domestic violence program had to decide whether to influence her abused client paternalistically (that is, discourage her from returning to her abusive husband) as a way to protect the client from herself.

The concept of paternalism is particularly complex for social workers because practitioners typically enter the profession because of their earnest, often passionate, wish to help people and protect them from harm. Intervention in people's lives is a core feature of the profession. In some important ways, not intervening in people's lives to protect them seems counterintuitive and contrary to the profession's principal mission. It is understandable that the social worker in this case had a natural instinct to want to persuade her client to not return to her husband, who had a significant history of abusive behavior.

Social workers need to be especially concerned about what I call *pseudopaternalism*. Pseudopaternalism occurs when social workers withhold information from clients, deceive clients, persuade clients, or interfere with clients and claim that these actions are necessary to protect clients, when in fact social workers engage in these actions to serve their own interests. For example, in case 2.2, pseudopaternalism would occur if the hospital-based social worker withheld truthful information from the patient about her cancer diagnosis and prognosis because the social worker was uncomfortable discussing these issues, claiming that he is withholding the information to protect the patient from emotional trauma. Another example involves a social worker who works for a community mental health center's program that serves people who are homeless. This social worker would behave pseudopaternalistically if she pressured a "difficult" client to go to an emergency shelter primarily because the social worker was tired of providing emergency services to this person in the community; this would be pseudopaternalistic if the social worker claimed that it was in the client's best interest to go to the shelter even though doing do was against the client's wishes. Pseudopaternalism in social work, where practitioners act in a manner that serves their own interests rather than clients', is unethical.

Social workers generally believe that they ought to respect clients' right to self-determination and avoid paternalism. This can be difficult, of course, particularly when social workers have reason to believe, based on their professional experience, that clients are engaging in risky behavior or using poor judgment that may harm themselves. In case 2.3, the social worker may believe that the client's judgment is not sound and that she would expose herself to serious risk if she returns to live with her abusive husband. The social worker is likely to feel caught between her wish to protect her client from harm and her wish to respect her client's right to self-determination and to assume risk. Consultation with colleagues and supervisors in this situation would be critically important.

It is understandable that most social workers find it hard to stand on the sidelines and watch while clients place themselves in harm's way. The social worker in case 2.2 did not want his vulnerable client to suffer emotional harm as a result of learning discouraging details about her health care status and prognosis. The social worker in case 2.3 did not want her client to be abused again by her husband. An enduring challenge for social workers is walking that fine line between respecting clients' right to self-determination, which may involve clients' exercising their right to make mistakes and assume risk, and intervening with clients against their wishes in an effort to protect them from harm.

In general, social workers should not interfere with clients paternalistically unless the practitioners have substantial and compelling evidence that clients pose a serious threat of harm to themselves. Thus, clients generally have the right to receive truthful responses from social workers about important matters in their lives, to refuse services, and to make their own choices so long as evidence indicates that they are making informed decisions voluntarily and with a clear understanding of possible consequences. Paternalism may be justifiable in extraordinary circumstances if clients are not mentally competent or if they would harm themselves seriously in some other way.

NASW *CODE OF ETHICS* STANDARDS: Commitment to Clients (1.01); Self-Determination (1.02); Informed Consent (1.03); Clients Who Lack Decision-Making Capacity (1.14); Consultation (2.05)

---

1. Think about clients with whom you are particularly interested in working (for example, victims of domestic violence or child molestation, people who struggle with substance abuse, elderly people, people who are clinically depressed or who have problems with anxiety). Are there any circumstances in which you can imagine interfering with your clients' right to self-determination by mandating services they do not want, withholding information from them, or providing them with false or misleading information? What are some examples?
2. To what extent do you think that clients have the right to engage in risky or self-harming behavior, without interference from social workers or others? Give examples.

Informed Consent

CASE 2.4. A social worker in independent (private) practice provided counseling services to a 29-year-old woman who has a significant trauma history. The client had been sexually abused as a child by her stepfather. For many years since then the woman has struggled with depression and has had difficulty in relationships.

The social worker suggested to the client that it might be helpful for her to engage in a series of therapeutic exercises that involve recreating the circumstances surrounding the client's sexual abuse victimization, as a way to "work through" the trauma. After three weeks of these exercises, the client was so traumatized that she attempted to commit suicide by overdosing on prescription medication.

Unfortunately, before beginning the exercises with the client, the social worker did not fully explain to the client the rationale behind these exercises and the risks involved, including the possibility that the client might become very distressed emotionally. The social worker also did not acquaint the client with therapeutic alternatives and their relative advantages and disadvantages.

CASE 2.5. A social worker in a middle school received a referral from the vice principal. The 12-year-old student, who had emigrated to the United States three years earlier from the Dominican Republic, had missed an unusually large number of school days and was struggling academically in several subjects. Two of the student's teachers reported that she seems remote and disengaged when she is in class. One teacher commented that the student seems to be depressed.

The social worker contacted the student's parents, whose primary language is Spanish. During his first meeting with the parents, the social worker sensed that the parents have difficulty communicating in English. The social worker did his best to explain the school staffers' concerns about their daughter and the social worker's plan to meet with her regularly to explore the issues in her life and help her get back on track. The social worker asked the parents for their permission to meet with their daughter and provide counseling; although the parents nodded their head "yes" when the social worker asked them for permission to meet with their daughter, the social worker was not convinced that the parents fully understood the points he made, the school's concerns, and the social worker's plans.

CASE 2.6. A social worker was employed in a vocational rehabilitation program affiliated with a major medical center. One of the social worker's clients, a 37-year-old man, has been diagnosed with traumatic brain injury and receives occupational therapy, physical therapy, speech and language, and counseling services from program staffers. The social worker helped the client cope with his feelings of despair and his increasing use of alcohol.

The social worker spoke with the client about her counseling goals and interventions, which include one-on-one counseling and group counseling with other clients who have experienced traumatic brain injury. The social worker also spoke with the client about the possibility of using some biofeedback techniques. However, the social worker was concerned that because of his brain injury the client did not fully understand her explanations, the intervention options, and possible benefits and risks.

CASE 2.7. The mother of a 10-year-old child contacted a social worker in independent (private) practice. The mother explained that her son has had a very difficult time coping with his parents' recent separation and impending divorce. According to the mother, the child has become quite sullen and defiant and expresses considerable anger, especially toward his father.

The social worker conducted a brief intake interview with the mother over the telephone and made an appointment to meet with her and the child. During their first meeting the social worker met with the child and the mother separately and then spoke with them together. The three agreed that the social worker would meet with the boy weekly.

Two months later the social worker received a telephone call from the boy's father, who just spent a weekend with his son and learned that the social worker has been counseling him. The father was enraged with the social worker and accused her of counseling his son behind the father's back. The father insisted that the social worker violated his rights by not contacting him about the counseling and obtaining his consent.

CASE 2.8. A social worker at a community mental health center met with a 47-year-old woman who had been ordered by the court to receive counseling. The woman had been arrested for shoplifting and cocaine possession. The criminal court judge placed the woman on probation with mandatory counseling.

The court's probation department referred the woman to the social worker's community mental health center. During the first counseling session the social worker talked with the woman about her obligations to the court, specifically the social worker's obligation to provide a report to the court about the client's progress and compliance with treatment. The social worker also spoke with the client about her limited right to confidentiality because of her status as a court-ordered, involuntary client.

During one clinical session the woman told the social worker that two days earlier she made a mistake at a friend's party and used a small amount of cocaine. The woman wanted to talk about how to resist this temptation in the future and prevent relapse. The social worker was unsure whether she had to report this information to the court.

CASE 2.9. A 42-year-old lawyer who lived in a small West Coast town struggled with depression and loneliness. His second marriage recently ended and he has had trouble adjusting to his new single life. The man is a public official and is well known locally. He was eager for counseling but, because of his concern about privacy, was uncomfortable seeking out the services of a local mental health professional.

The man read a newspaper article about a new and growing trend: counseling services via the Internet provided by social workers who are based all around the United States. After reading the article the man visited several Web sites to learn more about this option. He discovered that many clinical social workers and other mental health professionals offer online counseling services using e-mail. A typical clinical provider offers several counseling options, including telephone, live Internet chat, and e-mail communication. Some clinicians offer videoconferencing. Clients are charged by the hour for live chat or videoconferencing or by the number and length of e-mail messages. The man was intrigued by this innovative option, which offered appealing convenience and privacy, but he also had some concerns about the risks involved, especially because he would never meet his counselor in person.

CASE 2.10. A student in an MSW program was enrolled in an elective course on family intervention and therapy. The course provides students with an overview of diverse family intervention theories, models, and pertinent research evidence. One of the course assignments required students to videotape their work with a family with whom they are working as part of their internship in a mental health or family services agency.

As part of her internship, the student was working with a married couple and their two teenagers. The family was having a difficult time coping with the father's alcoholism and one of the teenager's drug use and defiant and aggressive behavior. In her work with the family, the student has been applying what she has learned about multisystemic family therapy. The student was eager to videotape two of her sessions with the family but was unsure of the best way to approach the family, address privacy and confidentiality issues, and obtain the family's consent.

Discussion

Social workers have always recognized the importance of informed consent, whether it pertains to the release of information, provision of services, medication, or audio or video recording. The current social work standard concerning informed consent reflects what professionals have learned about the nature of the consent process, particularly in light of various court decisions involving parties who questioned the validity of consent obtained by professionals.

A well-known legal ruling in the United States on informed consent is found in the 1914 landmark decision of *Schloendorff v. Society of New York Hospital*, in which New York Supreme Court Justice Benjamin Cardozo set forth his opinion concerning an individual's right to self-determination: "Every human being of adult years and sound mind has a right to determine what shall be done with his own body." To do otherwise, Cardozo argued, is to commit an assault upon the person.

Another key decision on informed consent was handed down in the 1957 case of *Salgo v. Leland Stanford Jr. University Board of Trustees*, in which the term "informed consent" was formally introduced. The plaintiff in this case, who became paraplegic following a diagnostic procedure for a circulatory problem, claimed that his physician did not properly disclose ahead of time pertinent information concerning risks associated with the procedure.

Thus, social workers who provided clinical services to clients are ethically obligated to obtain clients' informed consent. The social worker who provided services to the woman who had been sexually abused and who used controversial clinical techniques that may have harmed the client (case 2.4) had a duty to explain her clinical philosophy and methods, potential benefits and risks, alternative approaches, and so on. According to the NASW *Code of Ethics*:

> Social workers should provide services to clients only in the context of a professional relationship based, when appropriate, on valid informed consent. Social workers should use clear and understandable language to inform clients of the purpose of the services, risks related to the services, limits to services because of the requirements of a third-party payer, relevant costs, reasonable alternatives, clients' right to refuse or withdraw consent, and the time frame covered by the consent. Social workers should provide clients with an opportunity to ask questions. (standard 1.03[a])

Social workers also need to keep clients' unique circumstances in mind when obtaining clients' consent. For example, in case 2.5, the social worker was concerned that the parents' difficulty understanding English limited their ability to consent to the social worker's efforts to assist their struggling daughter. According to the NASW *Code of Ethics*,

> In instances when clients are not literate or have difficulty understanding the primary language used in the practice setting, social workers should take steps to ensure clients' comprehension. This may include providing clients with a detailed verbal explanation or arranging for a qualified interpreter or translator whenever possible. (standard 1.03[b])

Clients who have language difficulties would not be able to provide informed consent unless social workers take steps to ensure comprehension. Such steps include providing a detailed oral explanation to someone who is not literate or arranging for a qualified interpreter or translator when clients have difficulty understanding the primary language used in the practice setting. Social workers should be aware that some clients who are able to speak the primary language used in the practice setting (expressive language skill) may not be equally capable of understanding the language (receptive language skill).

Similarly, the social worker in case 2.6 must take special precautions to obtain consent to provide services to her client, a man whose competence is questionable because of his traumatic brain injury. This circumstance is addressed in the NASW *Code of Ethics*:

In instances when clients lack the capacity to provide informed consent, social workers should protect clients' interests by seeking permission from an appropriate third party, informing clients consistent with the clients' level of understanding. In such instances social workers should seek to ensure that the third party acts in a manner consistent with clients' wishes and interests. Social workers should take reasonable steps to enhance such clients' ability to give informed consent. (standard 1.03[c])

Social workers who deliver services to people with diminished capacity—for example, due to mental disability, mental illness, brain injury, or substance abuse—should attempt to obtain informed consent from an individual who is authorized to act on the client's behalf. This may be a relative, guardian, or some other individual who has legal authority to provide consent. Social workers must remember that, although clients may lack the capacity to provide informed consent (because of a permanent disability or temporary incapacity), clients retain the right to receive information about the purposes of consent consistent with their level of understanding and comprehension. Assessment of a client's capacity should include such measures as a mental status examination (evaluation of a person's orientation to person, place, time, situation, mood and affect, content of thought and perception), the ability to comprehend abstract ideas and make reasoned judgments, any history of mental illness that might affect current judgment, and the client's recent and remote memory. When clients are deemed incompetent, social workers should be guided by what is known as the principle of *substituted judgment* or *proxy judgment*, according to which an appropriate third party, or surrogate, attempts to replicate the decision that the incompetent client would make if able to make a sound decision.

Social workers who need to obtain informed consent from a third party for an incapacitated client also are obligated to enhance the client's ability to provide informed consent, when feasible. Sometimes little can be done to improve clients' capacity to provide informed consent, for example, when clients have suffered severe brain injury or have a severe mental disability. However, sometimes social workers may be able to enhance clients' ability to give informed consent, for example, when clients are hospitalized as a result of an acute episode of clinical depression or drug overdose. With appropriate services, these clients might very well regain their ability to provide informed consent without the formal involvement of a third party acting on their behalf.

Clients' competence to consent may be a function of legal criteria in addition to clinical criteria. For example, state laws vary considerably with regard to minors' right to consent to mental health and substance abuse treatment. In some states minors may have the legal right to consent. In other states minors may not have the legal authority to consent; in these instances social workers should at least seek minors' assent for services in an effort to promote these clients' right to self-determination (see case 2.7).

Some social work clients are mandated to receive services. Prominent examples include clients who are required by a judge to receive services as a condition of probation, as in case 2.8, or in parents' efforts to regain custody of a child, and clients who are incarcerated, hospitalized in a psychiatric facility, or court-ordered to receive social services as a condition of reunification with a child. When clients receive services involuntarily social workers should provide them with as much information as possible about the nature of the treatment or services they will receive and the extent of their right to refuse treatment and services. Consistent with the obligation to respect clients' right to socially responsible self-determination (see NASW *Code of Ethics* Standard 1.02), social workers should assist clients who wish to assert their right to refuse treatment or services, keeping in mind the simultaneous obligation to protect both clients and third parties from harm. Social workers may need to seek legal advice about any given client's right to refuse treatment or services. In these instances social workers have an ethical duty to explain to clients that ordinary informed consent guidelines do not pertain. According to the NASW *Code of Ethics,*

> In instances when clients are receiving services involuntarily, social workers should provide information about the nature and extent of services and about the extent of clients' right to refuse service. (standard 1.03[d])

The advent of modern electronic communication technology—voice-over-Internet telephone communication, e-mail, cell phone, fax machine—poses a number of unique ethical challenges. In case 2.9, for example, social workers who might provide counseling services via the Internet or long-distance telephone to the lawyer who was eager to arrange counseling but was concerned about his privacy need to be keenly concerned about complex issues related to informed consent, privacy, confidentiality, privileged communication, licensure, and liability. The MSW student who wants to videotape the family with which she is working (case 2.10) needs to be concerned about similar ethical issues. The NASW *Code of Ethics* addresses this issue:

> Social workers should take precautions to ensure and maintain the confidentiality of information transmitted to other parties through the use of computers, electronic mail, facsimile machines, telephones and telephone

answering machines, and other electronic or computer technology. Disclosure of identifying information should be avoided whenever possible. (standard 1.07[m])

Compliance with informed consent standards is particularly important when social workers communicate with clients and others electronically via e-mail, text message, fax machine, and videoconference. Practitioners who provide professional services by use of electronic media must be aware of and routinely inform recipients (who may or may not be formal clients) about the limitations and risks associated with such services. First, recipients should know that the information and advice they receive via electronic media may be superficial. E-mail responses to a client's complex clinical question, for example, may not always provide the same sort of useful detail that an in-person meeting would. Second, clients who receive clinical services via the Internet are not able to communicate important, informative visual cues to their social worker. Clinical social workers often find clients' behaviors during a clinical session, such as facial expressions or physically manifested agitation, meaningful in that they might interfere with the therapeutic alliance.

In addition, clients must be informed of potential privacy risks. Although Internet sites used for clinical purposes can be made rather secure, social workers cannot guarantee that there will be no invasions of privacy as a result of security breaches.

Federal and state jurisdictions and various professions (social work, psychology, marriage and family counseling, psychiatry, psychiatric nursing) have different interpretations of informed-consent standards, but there is considerable agreement about a number of key elements:

- Coercion and undue influence must not have played a role in the client's decision.
- Clients must be mentally capable of providing consent and able to understand the language and terms used during the consent process.
- Clients must consent to specific procedures or actions (such as clinical interventions, release of confidential information), not to broadly worded or blanket consent forms.
- The forms of consent must be valid (although some states require written authorization, most recognize both written and oral consent).
- Clients must have the right to refuse or withdraw consent.
- Clients' decision must be based on adequate information: details of the nature and purpose of a service or disclosure of information; advantages and disadvantages of an intervention; substantial or probable risks to clients, if

any; potential effects on clients' families, jobs, social activities, and other important aspects of their lives; alternatives to the proposed intervention or disclosure; and anticipated costs for clients and their relatives, if any. All this information must be presented to clients in understandable language and in a manner that encourages them to ask questions. Consent forms also should be dated and include an expiration date. Social workers should be especially sensitive to clients' cultural and ethnic differences related to the meaning of such concepts as "self-determination" and "consent."

NASW *Code of Ethics* standards: Commitment to Clients (1.01); Self-Determination (1.02); Informed Consent (1.03); Clients Who Lack Decision-Making Capacity (1.14); Consultation (2.05); Evaluation and Research (5.02)

Discussion questions

1. You are the newly appointed director of a private social service agency that provides counseling services to teenagers who are on probation. The youths you serve have been adjudicated delinquent by the local juvenile court and ordered to receive mental health counseling. What steps would you take to ensure that your agency complies with informed consent standards and clients' rights?

2. You are the clinical director of a counseling program that serves a large rural area. Many of your clients live long distances from your agency. You and your colleagues have decided to begin offering clients the opportunity to receive counseling services using videoconferencing and e-mail. What steps would you take to ensure that your agency complies with informed consent standards and clients' rights?

Practitioner Competence

Case 2.11. A 15-year-old high school student was referred by her student assistance counselor to a social worker at a nearby community mental health center. For several months the student's academic performance had been deteriorating; also, several teachers and the student assistance counselor reported that the student has been increasingly sullen and withdrawn.

For several months the social worker provided her client with supportive counseling and helped her cope with her feelings of depression. Recently the client lost a great deal of weight; her pediatrician contacted the social worker and expressed concerns about the possibility that the youngster was struggling with a serious eating disorder. The social worker, an MSW, had considerable clinical experience but did not have explicit training in the treatment of eating disorders.

CASE 2.12. A social worker in a family service agency provided counseling services to children and families. She specialized in children's behavioral issues and related parenting challenges; many of the children she served were referred by area schools that are concerned about the children's classroom behavior and academic performance.

The agency's clinical director, the social worker's immediate supervisor, informed the social worker that, because of a staffing shortage, the social worker would be assuming new responsibilities for the agency's adoption program. The social worker informed the clinical director that she had no formal training or expertise related to adoption. The clinical director told the social worker, "Don't worry—you're a quick study. You'll pick up what you need to know in no time." Despite this reassurance, the social worker questioned whether she was sufficiently knowledgeable about the unique and complicated clinical and legal issues related to adoption, such as counseling prospective adoptive parents, screening applicants and conducting home studies; navigating complex termination-of-parental-rights issues and interstate and international adoption issues; facilitating open adoptions; and helping families manage postadoption issues and crises.

CASE 2.13. A social worker in independent practice developed a unique clinical model for the treatment of trauma victims. The model included novel techniques that do not appear in widely used textbooks or educational curriculums, including various desensitization exercises, mind–body work, and intensive group retreats. The social worker developed a Web site promoting his treatment approach and publicizes it widely.

Discussion

It may go without saying that social workers should provide services to clients only when they have the requisite competence and expertise. Sometimes there is a clear line between sufficient expertise and lack of expertise. Social workers whose education focused exclusively on policy issues or community organizing should not provide clinical services. Social workers with extensive clinical expertise should not claim to be expert researchers or program evaluators if their training and education did not focus on these areas.

But once we move beyond these obvious delineations, we quickly encounter ambiguity. How much explicit training and education on the subject of eating disorders, beyond general clinical training and education, are necessary to help a client who is struggling with these symptoms in addition to other symptoms that are more in line with the social worker's competence and expertise? To what extent can a social worker who has served as director of a clinical program claim to be a competent administrator, even though her formal education did not include any courses on agency administration?

Because often there are no formal criteria to establish professional competence (beyond certification or licensure), social workers bear the burden of being forthright in their claims about their areas of expertise to clients, the public at large, colleagues, and employers. Practitioners must not misrepresent their competence for self-serving purposes to attract clients or gain employment. For example, the social worker in case 2.11 would assume considerable risk if she sought to treat her client's apparent eating disorder entirely on her own. Clients who struggle with an eating disorder can suffer great physical harm, even mortality, if they do not receive skilled, competent treatment from clinicians with specialized knowledge and expertise. According to the NASW *Code of Ethics*,

> Social workers should provide services and represent themselves as competent only within the boundaries of their education, training, license, certification, consultation received, supervised experience, or other relevant professional experience. (standard 1.04[a])

On occasion, as in case 2.12, a social worker's agency will place her or him in a position for which he or she does not have adequate expertise. This can occur when an agency is short-staffed or having difficulty hiring someone better suited to the unique position. In these instances, social workers have an ethical obligation to convey their concerns to administrators and seek reasonable alternatives. According to the NASW *Code of Ethics*,

> Social workers should provide services in substantive areas or use intervention techniques or approaches that are new to them only after engaging in appropriate study, training, consultation, and supervision from people who are competent in those interventions or techniques. (standard 1.04[b])

Different ethical issues arise when social workers seek to use clinical or other intervention protocols that are widely considered to be controversial or untested, as in case 2.13. Not all intervention innovations are controversial; some cutting-edge innovations find their way into mainstream professional practice fairly quickly. Others, however, though embraced by a small percentage of practitioners, labor under a cloud of suspicion and skepticism. In these instances social workers are unable to point to generally recognized standards that guide practice. Social workers who choose to use novel intervention protocols would do well to spend considerable time reading the relevant literature, consulting with colleagues, attending workshops and continuing education seminars, and obtaining appropriate supervision. According to the NASW *Code of Ethics*,

> When generally recognized standards do not exist with respect to an emerging area of practice, social workers should exercise careful judgment and take responsible steps (including appropriate education, research, training, consultation, and supervision) to ensure the competence of their work and to protect clients from harm. (standard 1.04[c])

Even with these safeguards in place, social workers assume considerable risk, and may expose clients to significant risk, when they use controversial interventions.

NASW *CODE OF ETHICS* STANDARDS: Commitment to Clients (1.01); Informed Consent (1.03); Competence (1.04 and 4.01); Consultation (2.05); Referral for Services (2.06); Incompetence of Colleagues (2.10); Misrepresentation (4.06)

DISCUSSION QUESTIONS

1. You are a social worker at a community mental health center. You provide counseling services to clients with persistent and chronic mental illness, such as schizophrenia and bipolar disorder. One day the clinical director of the agency informs you that your position has been expanded to include facilitating a treatment group with clients who have been diagnosed with co-occurring symptoms of mental illness and substance abuse (also known as dual diagnosis). You feel ill equipped to facilitate this treatment group; you have never received any formal education or training on the subject of co-occurring disorders and dual diagnoses. How would you respond to the news about your redefined duties at the agency? What steps would you take?

2. You are the social worker in case 2.11. You want to continue working with your adolescent client who is clinically depressed and seems to be struggling with an eating disorder. What steps would you take to decide whether to continue treating this client or refer the client to a colleague?

Cultural Competence and Social Diversity

CASE 2.14. A social worker in a public child welfare agency provided casework services to children who have been abused and neglected. Many of the social worker's clients live in foster homes and group homes. One of the social worker's clients was a 15-year-old boy who was physically abused and has run away from several foster homes. The boy disclosed to the social worker that he is gay.

During a conversation with her supervisor, the social worker explained that, "as a person of faith, I have a hard time working with a client who lives a gay lifestyle. In my religion, that's a sin. I really feel strongly that what's best for this boy is to know the Lord." The supervisor was unsure about how to respond.

CASE 2.15. A 10-year-old child was referred to his school's social worker by the student's teacher. The teacher noticed bruising on the child's arms. The social worker interviewed the child and learned that the child's parents occasionally place a heated cup on his body or scrape a coin across it when he is ill. The child, who is the son of Cambodian immigrants, explained to the social worker that many Cambodian children are treated this way. The social worker consulted with a Cambodian colleague, who explained that these methods of "cupping" and "coining" are considered traditional forms of healing. The social worker was concerned about the marks left on the child's body and whether he should consult with state protective services officials.

CASE 2.16. A social worker was employed at a rehabilitation facility that serves clients who have serious physical disabilities. The parents of one of the social worker's clients, an 11-year-old girl, shared with the social worker that they sleep with their daughter. The social worker expressed surprise and shared her concern about the sleeping arrangement. The parents explained that in their native culture it is common for children to sleep with their parents.

Discussion

One of the most significant developments in social work has been professionals' understanding and appreciation of the relevance of cultural competence and social diversity. In recent years social workers have developed an impressive appreciation of the complex ways in which clients' cultures, ethnic backgrounds, disabilities, and sexual orientation affect practice. Social workers now have a fuller understanding of the ways in which culture, ethnicity, and other forms of diversity influence how people cope with life's problems and relationships with professional helpers. The ways in which clients understand and cope with the death of a loved one, a family member's or their own mental illness, and their management of boundaries in relationships with social workers may be a function of deep-seated cultural beliefs and values. For example, some clients may believe that they can communicate with deceased relatives or that mental illness is punishment for their behavior in a past life.

Also, clients' cultural backgrounds may influence their willingness to seek help from, and trust, social workers. Some cultural groups may prefer informal, community-based aid from neighbors, friends, and relatives; some people who have felt oppressed or exploited in the past may not trust social workers or other professionals who are in positions of authority.

In addition, the ways in which social workers design and implement programs and services may affect their effectiveness with particular cultural groups. Cultural and ethnic norms related to confidentiality and boundaries, for example, vary; programs that insist on strict boundaries between clients and staffers may appeal to some groups of clients and alienate others because of differences in their cultural practices, values, and beliefs.

Social workers face unique challenges when clients' or colleagues' cultural beliefs clash with the social worker's or the profession's values. For example, in case 2.14 the social worker, who had strong religious beliefs about the immorality of homosexuality, was uncomfortable with her client's sexual orientation. In this instance, the social work profession's standards regarding acceptance of clients' diversity clashed with the social worker's personal values. The task for the social worker's supervisor is to help the social worker distinguish between her personal values and the profession's values and grasp how, in the end, the social worker must respect the client's preferences, even if the social worker does not embrace them. The social worker in this case needs to develop a clearer understanding of boundary issues that arise in work with clients whose values are different from her own.

In case 2.15 the social worker also encountered client behavior that was unfamiliar and troubling to the social worker, who was concerned that the parents' traditional healing practices may be abusive. In this instance, the social worker had a duty to educate himself about these cultural practices and consult with informed colleagues who could help the social worker understand that they are not abusive. The social worker should be sensitive to the parents' culture and may also want to explore constructive ways to help them learn about resources available in their community and how they may be useful to the family. According to the NASW *Code of Ethics,*

Social workers should understand culture and its function in human behavior and society, recognizing the strengths that exist in all cultures. (standard 1.05[a])

Social workers should have a knowledge base of their clients' cultures and be able to demonstrate competence in the provision of services that are sensitive to clients' cultures and to differences among people and cultural groups. (standard 1.05[b])

Social workers should obtain education about and seek to understand the nature of social diversity and oppression with respect to race, ethnicity, national origin, color, sex, sexual orientation, age, marital status, political belief, religion, and mental or physical disability. (standard 1.05[c])

The circumstances in case 2.16 pose a different kind of ethical challenge. In this case the social worker is concerned about the parents who reported sleeping with their preadolescent child. In this case it is reasonable for the social worker to explore whether the parents' behavior is culturally appropriate and does not constitute child abuse (that is, sleeping with one's child is culturally normative for this family and does not involve any sexual contact) or, rather, is abusive. Consultation with colleagues who are familiar with the family's culture and colleagues who have expertise related to protective services (child abuse, in particular) would be important.

NASW *CODE OF ETHICS* STANDARDS: Commitment to Clients (1.01); Self-Determination (1.02); Informed Consent (1.03); Competence (1.04 and 4.01); Cultural Competence and Social Diversity (1.05); Consultation (2.05); Referral for Services (2.06)

DISCUSSION QUESTIONS:

1. You are a social worker in a family services agency. The agency's clients are very diverse racially and ethnically. The agency director asks you to develop a staff development workshop that will acquaint employees with key issues related to cultural competence and diversity. What issues would you address? What would you include in this workshop?

2. You are a social worker in a pediatric hospital. You receive a referral involving a child who is suffering from a life-threatening infection. The child's doctors have recommended a blood transfusion. The child's parents explain to you that their religion prohibits blood transfusions; they refuse to consent to a transfusion. Would you respect the family's religious beliefs or would you take steps to override their wishes?

Conflicts of Interest

CASE 2.17. A social worker in a community mental health center in a large city was working with a client who struggles with clinical depression and anxiety. Over time the social worker had become concerned about the client's apparent alcohol abuse. The social worker told the client that he is worried that the client is using alcohol to "self-medicate" his depression and anxiety symptoms. The social worker encouraged the client to explore Alcoholics Anonymous (AA) meetings to address his drinking problems. After a traumatic weekend during which he became drunk and abusive toward his partner, the client decided to attend an AA meeting in a nearby church. Shortly after he arrived at the meeting room, the client was surprised to see his social worker in attendance. Upon seeing his client, the social worker briefly acknowledged that he, the social worker, also is in recovery; the social worker told the client that they would discuss their unexpected encounter at their next regularly scheduled counseling session. The social worker was unsure about how to best manage the boundary issues that just emerged.

CASE 2.18. A social worker in a small rural town (population 5,650) provided crisis intervention and counseling services to area residents. She was one of only two licensed mental health professionals in town. One of her clients was the local grade school's fourth-grade teacher. The teacher sought counseling to address chronic marital issues.

In the middle of the school year the teacher was informed that she would be responsible for a combined third- and fourth-grade classroom; the school's third-grade teacher had died suddenly and the school's principal decided to combine the third and fourth grades, both of which had low enrollments, for the remainder of the school year.

Coincidentally, the social worker's own son was enrolled in the school's third grade. To complicate matters, the social worker's son was struggling with serious behavioral issues, about which the social worker had been consulting with the teacher who died and with the school's principal. The social worker was not sure how to sort through the complex boundary and conflict of interest issues involving her relationship with her client, who was also her child's new teacher.

CASE 2.19. A social worker in a hospital emergency department provided crisis intervention services to trauma patients. One of the social worker's clients was a 38-year-old man who was brought to the hospital by rescue after being severely injured in an automobile accident; the man's wife died in the accident. The man was in severe pain and learned that a hospital surgeon would need to amputate his left leg. The social worker spent about 25 minutes with the man in an effort to console him and help him deal with his traumatic injuries and impending amputation. The man was distraught and very anxious.

Nearly four years later the social worker and the man recognized each other at a backyard party hosted by an acquaintance they shared in common. The two spent time that evening recalling the events of the man's traumatic injury and hospital experience. The social worker was heartened by the man's report that he was coping reasonably well since the accident that killed his wife and severely injured him. By the end of the evening the social worker, who was single, and the man acknowledged that they enjoyed each other's company and would like to get together again. On her way home, the social worker began to wonder about becoming involved with a man to whom she had provided very intense, albeit very brief, clinical services.

CASE 2.20. A social worker in private practice worked with a 17-year-old boy who had a difficult adolescence. The boy, who was adopted at age 7 after his stepfather and mother had abused him physically, lived in foster care. The boy was referred to the social worker nearly three years ago after he cut his wrists in a suicide attempt. The boy was diagnosed with posttraumatic stress disorder, clinical depression, and anxiety.

During the past year the boy made remarkable clinical progress. He began to excel in school, after years of poor academic performance, and develop healthy relationships for the first time in his life.

At the conclusion of his most recent counseling session, the boy and his foster mother handed the social worker an envelope and a small box. The social worker opened them and discovered that the family had given her a necklace and an invitation to the boy's high school graduation and a post-ceremony party at the family's home. The boy's foster mother said to the social worker, "You know, you're the one who made all this possible. We can't begin to tell you what a difference you've made in Carlos's life, and ours. This is just a small token of appreciation. It would mean so much to us if you would join us for the graduation events."

Discussion

This diverse cross-section of cases has one key element in common: Each one contains an actual or potential conflict of interest. Ethical issues involving conflicts of interest are among the most complex and challenging faced by social workers. Conflicts of interest occur when a social worker's services to or relationship with a client is compromised, or might be compromised, because of decisions in relation to another client, a colleague, herself or himself, or some other third party. Conflicts of interest may be actual or potential (when conflicting interests may develop but do not yet exist).

Social workers must be careful to avoid conflicts of interest that might harm clients because of their decisions or actions involving other clients, colleagues, themselves, or other third parties. In social work, conflicts of interest can take several forms. As in case 2.17, where the social worker who is in recovery encountered a client at an AA meeting, conflicts of interest can arise when practitioners encounter clients outside of the office and in a setting that reveals personal information about the social worker. In other instances, particularly in small or rural communities, social workers' and clients' paths may intersect in ways that complicate their relationship, as in case 2.18, where the social worker's child has special needs and is a student in the social worker's client's classroom. In both of these cases, the social workers must be sensitive to what it means for clients to learn very personal information about their social worker's life and the potential implications for their clinical relationship.

Conflict of interest issues can also arise in social workers' relationships with former clients, as in case 2.19, where the social worker and the former hospital patient encountered each other quite by happenstance years after their brief contact at the hospital. Complex issues also emerge when clients invite social workers into their personal lives, as in case 2.20, where the teenager and his foster family were eager for the social worker to attend the teenager's high school graduation and the post-ceremony party at the family's home. Another example involves social workers in administrative positions who consider hiring a former client as a staffer, for example, when a client who is in substance abuse recovery applies for a job in a program where he had been a client. On the one hand, hiring a former client who understands the nature of the helping relationship and the program's unique features can strengthen a program's services; on the other hand, hiring a former client can lead to boundary challenges when former clients have access to confidential information about people they knew when they were clients in the same program, when the former client is supervised as an employee by a staffer with whom he or she once had a therapeutic relationship, and when the former client and his or her former clinician begin to socialize as colleagues. Managing these dual relationships in ways that prevent harm to the former client, who is now a colleague, can be very difficult, albeit not impossible.

41

When potential or actual conflicts of interest arise, social workers are obligated to handle the conflict in a way that minimizes possible harm. As the NASW *Code of Ethics* states,

> Social workers should be alert to and avoid conflicts of interest that interfere with the exercise of professional discretion and impartial judgment. Social workers should inform clients when a real or potential conflict of interest arises and take reasonable steps to resolve the issue in a manner that makes the clients' interests primary and protects clients' interests to the greatest extent possible. In some cases, protecting clients' interests may require termination of the professional relationship with proper referral of the client. (standard 1.06[a])

> Social workers should not take unfair advantage of any professional relationship or exploit others to further their personal, religious, political, or business interests. (standard 1.06[b])

In light of these ethical standards, the social worker in case 2.17 needs to set aside time to discuss with his client the implications of their encounter at the AA meeting. Their simultaneous attendance at the meeting introduces a potential conflict of interest. The social worker's presence at the meeting may confuse the client about the nature of their relationship and, possibly, could interfere with the client's clinical progress. The social worker would need to decide whether it is appropriate for him and the client to attend future 12-step meetings together, in light of the potential risk to the client, and whether, if the social worker and client are likely to encounter each other at future meetings, the social worker should find an alternative AA meeting or refer the client to another practitioner. Similarly, the social worker in case 2.18, whose own child is now her client's student, must discuss the potential conflict of interest with her client and assess whether it would be best to refer the client to another practitioner. One practical challenge in small, rural communities is that referral options may be limited or, in some cases, nonexistent.

The emergency department social worker who encountered the former trauma patient unexpectedly at a backyard party (case 2.19) needs to think carefully about whether a social relationship is likely to harm the client and whether such a relationship is likely to be exploitive. On its face, such a relationship, in light of these unusual circumstances and the social worker's and client's remarkably brief and limited encounter at the hospital, seems unlikely to pose a significant risk.

In contrast, the social worker who was invited to her client's graduation and post-ceremony party may need to set firmer limits (case 2.20). Attending the graduation may be reasonable, assuming that the social worker protects the client's privacy and confidentiality when she encounters other guests. The social worker may want to explain to the client that she will attend the graduation ceremony and the reasons why, avoid mingling with other guests, and not attend the post-ceremony party because of the social work profession's norms pertaining to social contact between practitioners and clients. Also, the social worker will need to talk with the clients about the gift. On the one hand, accepting the gift would honor the family's understandable wish to express their gratitude and appreciation. On the other hand, accepting the gift could complicate the social worker's relationship with the client by suggesting that it has evolved into a friendship.

Boundary issues also arise when social workers consider giving clients gifts or performing favors for them. For example, in one case a social worker in a shelter for people who are homeless gave a client the social worker's winter coat that he no longer used. The client was deeply appreciative and began to regard the social worker as a friend. Complex boundary issues emerged when the social worker tried to set limits in their relationship. The social worker realized, too late, that his innocent, altruistic gesture was misinterpreted. After consulting with colleagues about managing the boundary issues, the social worker learned that he could have avoided the boundary issue by donating his old winter coat to his agency and letting his client know that the agency maintains a clothes closet with lots of donated articles. The social worker could have matched the client with the winter coat the social worker had donated without framing it as a personal gift. This would have defused the boundary issue. Sometimes simple and creative options—such as donating one's extra clothing items to one's agency rather than giving them directly to clients as gifts—help social workers to avoid complex, troublesome boundary problems.

These cases raise complex issues related to professional boundaries and dual or multiple relationships. Dual or multiple relationships assume many forms in social work; some are ethically problematic and some are not. At one extreme are dual and multiple relationships that are not inherently unethical, such as encountering a client unexpectedly at the supermarket or discovering that a client's employer is the social worker's former college roommate from years ago. These situations may require skilled, careful management to avoid boundary problems and protect clients but they are not, in and of themselves, high-risk ethics circumstances. This is not to say that an unexpected client encounter or boundary issue should be ignored, but this sort of circumstance is not likely to stir up complex clinical issues or lead to major harm.

At the other extreme are dual or multiple relationships that pose significant risk and raise serious ethical questions. Egregious examples involve social workers who become sexually involved with a client, develop a business relationship with a current client, or travel on vacation with a client. In these instances there is likely exploitation of or potential harm to the client. The dual relationship could adversely affect the social worker's clinical objectivity and judgment; also, the boundary violation may undermine the client's trust in the social worker and confuse the client about the social worker's role in her or his life.

When social workers encounter challenging boundary issues they should consult with colleagues and supervisors to assess the circumstances, clinical and other implications, and pertinent ethical standards. Some dual and multiple relationships are more avoidable than others. Entering into sexual and business relationships with clients is avoidable; inadvertent encounters with clients in small and rural communities may not be.

In some instances social workers may discover that knowledgeable and principled colleagues and supervisors disagree among themselves with regard to the "right" course of action; however, competent, skilled consultation and supervision can enhance the protection of clients and minimize risk. In every instance, social workers should carefully examine their own motives and needs and how they are relevant to the boundary issue. In many cases involving inappropriate and harmful dual relationships, social workers fail to examine or recognize their self-serving motives or interests and are not sufficiently attuned to the complex ways in which clients may be harmed. Furthermore, social workers who are drawn into inappropriate dual relationships with clients often fail to recognize how publicity about these relationships damages the social work profession's integrity and public perception of social workers.

In all instances, when social workers encounter complex boundary or dual relationship issues, their principal goal should be to minimize potential harm to clients. According to the NASW *Code of Ethics*,

> Social workers should not engage in dual or multiple relationships with clients or former clients in which there is a risk of exploitation or potential harm to the client. In instances when dual or multiple relationships are unavoidable, social workers should take steps to protect clients and are responsible for setting clear, appropriate, and culturally sensitive boundaries.

(Dual or multiple relationships occur when social workers relate to clients in more than one relationship, whether professional, social, or business. Dual or multiple relationships can occur simultaneously or consecutively.) (standard 1.06[c])

NASW *Code of Ethics* standards: Commitment to Clients (1.01); Informed Consent (1.03); Conflicts of Interest (1.06); Sexual Relationships (1.09); Physical Contact (1.10); Sexual Harassment (1.11); Consultation (2.05); Referral for Services (2.06); Unethical Conduct of Colleagues (2.11); Impairment (4.05)

Discussion questions

1. You are a social worker in a high school. You provide counseling and crisis intervention to students. You have developed a good working relationship with a student who has had difficulty coping with his parents' divorce and has been smoking marijuana frequently. During one of your conversations the student asks you whether you smoked marijuana when you were his age. How would you respond to the question? Under what circumstances would you feel comfortable sharing personal information about yourself? How would you decide whether to share personal information with your clients?
2. You are a social worker in a HIV/AIDS clinic. One of your clients, whom you have known for nearly two years, is gravely ill and is expected to die within several weeks. One morning the client tells you how much you have meant to him and that he has decided to include you in his will. How would you respond?
3. You are a social worker in private practice. One of your clients, the mother of two young children, is struggling with marital issues; one of the client's children has been diagnosed with a serious developmental disability. Several months after you began working with the client, you encounter the client unexpectedly at the first meeting of a weekly support group for parents of children with developmental disabilities; you attended the meeting, which was held in one of the group members' homes, because one of your children has a developmental disability. How would you manage the boundary issues?

Privacy and Confidentiality

Case 2.21. A social worker in a community mental health center provided counseling to a 43-year-old man who had an on-again, off-again relationship with a woman he has known for about six years. Two years earlier the woman had called the police about the man, alleging that he had physically assaulted her. The client was charged with domestic assault, went to trial, and was sentenced to six months in jail and required to enroll in domestic violence counseling upon his release. Eventually the woman petitioned the court to lift the no-contact order that it had put in place and the couple reconciled.

About a year ago the man sought counseling with the social worker to help him address issues he was dealing with related to depression, alcohol abuse, and conflict with his partner. During one clinical session the client seemed unusually despondent and angry. He told the social worker that he was "sick and tired" of all of the problems in his life, which he blamed mostly on his partner. The man became increasingly agitated as he told the social worker about how he knows his partner has been unfaithful with one of the man's coworkers. At one point in the conversation the man blurted out, "I just can't stand that woman any longer. She's been nothing but trouble. I just may have to get rid of her and that no-good former buddy of mine who's been sleeping with her."

CASE 2.22. A social worker in a family service agency provided counseling services to adolescents. One of the social worker's clients was a 15-year-old boy who was coping with clinical depression. The boy had been having lots of conflict with his parents, staying out after curfew, and struggling in school. The boy's parents were worried that they were losing their son; they were especially worried about new friends he has made, mostly teenagers who have dropped out of school.

The boy arrived at a clinical session with blurred eyes and slurred speech. In response to the social worker's question about his condition, the boy admitted that he was under the influence and that his new friends have introduced him to new drugs like ecstasy and crystal meth. The boy told the social worker that he knows he is in "deep trouble" and is worried about his escalating drug use. The social worker told the boy that she can enroll him in the agency's state-funded program for adolescents who have both mental health and substance abuse challenges. The boy agreed to participate in the program but refused to allow the social worker to tell his parents about his drug problem. The social worker did not know whether she was allowed to provide the boy with drug counseling without informing his parents and obtaining their consent.

CASE 2.23. A social worker at a psychiatric day-treatment program facilitated a support group for clients who are HIV-positive. The group provides an opportunity for clients to talk about the unique challenges they face. During one group session one of the clients, a 35-year-old man who contracted HIV through the use of dirty needles when he was a heroin user, talked about his "wonderful" relationship with a woman he knows from his neighborhood. The client acknowledged that he has not told his girlfriend, with whom he has been sexually involved, that he is HIV-positive. The client told the group that he loves his girlfriend "more than anything" and that he knows he needs to tell her about his health status. The client explained that he "just needs some time to figure out the best way to do this; I'm so afraid she'll leave me once she finds out." The social worker offered to help the client figure out how to share this information with his girlfriend, but the client rejected the offer. The social worker was very anxious about the risk to the client's girlfriend and unsure about how to handle the conflict between her client's right to confidentiality and her duty to protect third parties from harm.

CASE 2.24. A social worker who was a case manager at a shelter for the homeless was called to the front desk by the shelter's receptionist. A police detective was at the front desk and wanted to speak to the social worker about a murder investigation. The detective explained to the social worker that a police officer found a jacket near the unidentified victim's body that had a piece of paper in the pocket with the social worker's name and telephone number. The police detective showed the social worker a photograph of the victim and asked the social worker whether he recognized the person in the photo. The social worker was unsure about whether to tell the detective that, indeed, the person in the photo has been a guest at the shelter and whether to share the man's name.

CASE 2.25. A social worker in a family services agency provided counseling to an 11-year-old girl whose mother was very concerned about her defiant behavior at home and deteriorating school grades. The mother brought her daughter to the social worker after receiving a referral from the school guidance counselor. The social worker provided counseling to the girl and, occasionally, her mother for about three months.

One afternoon the social worker received a telephone call from the girl's father, who lived in another state. The girl's parents were in the midst of divorce proceedings and a custody dispute. The father asked the social worker for a copy of the social worker's clinical record and notes. The father said that his lawyer wanted to see the clinical record. The social worker was unsure about whether the father should have access to the confidential clinical record.

47

CASE 2.26. A social worker recently started a job as a clinician at a residential program for adolescent girls. About two weeks after the job started, the social worker attended a regularly scheduled staff meeting to review new referrals. The purpose of the meeting was to review records and clinical information of girls who have been referred for admission to the group home.

One of the teenagers being reviewed was a 15-year-old girl who was in foster care as a result of parental abuse and neglect. The girl struggled with serious behavioral issues; at times she was defiant and argumentative and abused drugs and alcohol.

Shortly after the staffers began to discuss the girl, the social worker realized that she knew the girl from her previous job as a caseworker with the agency that runs the foster care program that supervises the girl's current foster placement. The social worker knew that earlier the girl had been arrested on arson charges and that the matter was pending in juvenile court. However, none of the information about the arson charges was included in the material available to the residential program staffers who were considering the girl for admission.

The social worker knew that the residential program has a policy that prohibits admission of teenagers who have a history with arson. The social worker had to decide whether to share with her current colleagues the confidential information she had about the girl's arson charges; the social worker did not have authorization to release this information, which she knew only through her prior employment in the foster care program.

Discussion

Privacy and confidentiality are bedrock principles in social work practice. In clinical contexts, clients' willingness to trust social workers depends on their belief that social workers will respect their privacy and honor confidentiality. Clients who have doubts about social workers' commitment to client privacy and confidentiality are likely to be reluctant to share sensitive information about their lives.

There are several sets of circumstances in which social workers are in a position to disclose confidential information. First, clients may initiate requests for social workers to release confidential information to a third party. For example, a client may ask a social worker to disclose confidential information to an attorney who represents the client in a custody or divorce proceeding. Second, social workers may receive requests for confidential information from third parties. For example, a police detective may ask a social worker for confidential information in conjunction with a criminal investigation (as in case 2.24) or the parent of a minor client, or her or his attorney, may ask the social worker to share confidential information about her or his child (as in case 2.25). In other instances social workers may wrestle with whether they have a duty to disclose confidential information to protect third parties (as in cases 2.21 and 2.23).

In general, social workers should disclose confidential information only when they have obtained valid consent from the client or a person legally authorized to consent on the client's behalf (there may be exceptions in emergency circumstances or when a judge orders a social worker to release confidential records). When social workers request clients' consent, they should use clear and understandable language to inform clients of the purpose of the consent and the disclosure, the risks related to the disclosure, reasonable alternatives (if any), the client's right to refuse or withdraw consent, and the time frame covered by the consent. Social workers also should provide clients with an opportunity to ask questions about the consent to disclose confidential information.

Many requests for confidential information received by social workers are straightforward. For example, when a client's psychiatrist asks her social worker for a progress report, a brief conversation between the social worker and client and the client's consent easily addresses the request.

However, in other situations managing client confidentiality is much more complicated. Social workers need to think very carefully about circumstances that warrant disclosure of confidential information, without client consent, to protect third parties (as in cases 2.21, 2.23, and 2.26); disclosure to law enforcement officials (as in case 2.24); and disclosure to parents of minor clients (as in case 2.22 and 2.25).

Social workers have access to well-established guidelines concerning disclosures of confidential information, without client consent, to protect third parties. These guidelines are rooted in the precedent-setting case of *Tarasoff v. Board of Regents of the University of California* (1976). In 1969 Prosenjit Poddar, an outpatient at Cowell Memorial Hospital at the University of California at Berkeley, informed his psychologist, Dr. Lawrence Moore, that he was planning to kill an unnamed young woman (easily identified as Tatiana Tarasoff) on her return to the university from her summer vacation. After the counseling session during which Poddar announced his plan, Moore notified the university police and asked them to observe Poddar because he might need hospitalization as an individual who was dangerous to himself or others. The psychologist followed the telephone call with a letter requesting the help of the chief of the university police.

The campus police temporarily took Poddar into custody but released him because there was evidence that he was rational. They also warned him to stay away from Tarasoff. Poddar then moved in with Tarasoff's brother in an apartment near Tarasoff's home, where she lived with her parents. Shortly thereafter, Moore's supervisor and the chief of the department of psychiatry, Dr. Harvey Powelson, asked the university police to return the psychologist's letter about Poddar, ordered that the letter and the psychologist's case notes be destroyed, and directed that no further action be taken to hospitalize Poddar. No one warned Tarasoff or her family of Poddar's threat. Poddar never returned to counseling. Two months later, he murdered Tarasoff.

Tarasoff's parents sued the university board of regents, several employees of the student health service, and the chief of the campus police, along with four of his officers, because their daughter was never notified of Poddar's threat. A lower court in California dismissed the suit on the basis of sovereign immunity of the multiple defendants and the psychotherapist's need to preserve confidentiality. The parents appealed, and the California Supreme Court upheld the appeal and later reaffirmed the appellate court's decision that failure to protect Tarasoff, Poddar's intended victim, was irresponsible.

Without question, *Tarasoff* changed the way social workers and other mental health professionals think about the limits of clients' right to confidentiality. Since the *Tarasoff* decision, a number of important duty-to-protect cases have influenced courts, legislatures, and mental health professions. Many court decisions reinforce the California court's conclusions in *Tarasoff*, emphasizing practitioners' responsibility to take reasonable steps to protect third parties when, in the professional's judgment, clients' actions or potential actions pose a serious, foreseeable, and imminent risk to others. These various guidelines are reflected in the NASW *Code of Ethics*:

> Social workers should protect the confidentiality of all information obtained
> in the course of professional service, except for compelling professional rea-
> sons. The general expectation that social workers will keep information
> confidential does not apply when disclosure is necessary to prevent serious,
> foreseeable, and imminent harm to a client or other identifiable person. In
> all instances, social workers should disclose the least amount of confidential
> information necessary to achieve the desired purpose; only information that
> is directly relevant to the purpose for which the disclosure is made should
> be revealed. (standard 1.07[c])

These guidelines are widely accepted and implemented in cases where angry and agitated clients threaten to harm a third party, such as a spouse, partner, coworker, or supervisor, with a gun, knife, or other form of physical assault. However, there is less clarity about some unique circumstances, particularly those involving HIV-infected clients, as in case 2.23. These situations provide an important reminder that even the clearest ethics guidelines do not necessarily provide unambiguous guidance in complex situations.

In case 2.23 the social worker used various clinical approaches in an attempt to bring the client to a point at which he was willing to inform his partner about his medical condition. Unfortunately, this clinical strategy did not succeed and the social worker had to decide whether to disclose confidential information against the client's wishes and take steps to ensure that the sexual partner was informed of the potential risk (including the possibility that she was already infected).

This social worker faced a complex, daunting ethical dilemma. The social worker had to decide whether to respect the client's wish for confidentiality and privacy or disclose confidential information to protect a third party. The social worker felt as if she had exhausted all the clinical options to help the client reach a point at which he was willing to share the information with his partner. However, unlike *Tarasoff*-like cases, in which clients threaten to harm a third party, in this HIV case the client claimed to love his partner, did not plan to harm her, and simply needed time to figure out the best way to share this information. In that respect, the social worker may not have had sufficient evidence to demonstrate that, as the NASW *Code of Ethics* says, "disclosure is necessary to prevent serious, foreseeable, and imminent harm to a client or other identifiable person." One can certainly understand that, in the social worker's judgment, the client's partner was at risk of exposure to HIV. The question is whether the social worker had sufficient evidence to satisfy the social work profession's ethical standard and standards established under the law.

A number of states now have statutes that permit disclosure by a physician of HIV-related confidential information to protect a third party if the physician (not a social worker, psychologist, counselor, or psychiatric nurse) believes that disclosure is necessary to prevent harm and the physician has provided the patient (client) with information about the need to disclose and has reason to believe that the patient (client) has not disclosed and does not plan to disclose. Case 2.23 is particularly important because, on its face, it requires what for many social workers is counterintuitive thinking. The bare facts of the case suggest to many social workers that its circumstances fall within widely accepted "duty to protect" guidelines established by the *Tarasoff* case and subsequent court cases. However, a close reading of these duty-to-protect guidelines suggests that the particular circumstances in case 2.23—especially the client's claim that he loves his girlfriend and does not want to harm her—may not satisfy the strict criteria required for disclosure without client consent. Moreover, the statutory requirements contained in many state laws prohibit disclosure by any professional other than a physician.

The circumstances in case 2.26 also pose a unique challenge. In this case, the social worker was aware of confidential information about the client's pending arson charges which, because the client is a minor, are not a matter of public record. The social worker was privy to this information from her prior employment with the agency that is supervising the teenager's foster care. The social worker did not have permission to share this information with her current colleagues in the residential program that is considering this teenager for admission. Without the client's (or a parent or guardian's) consent or a court order, the social worker would need to review standards in the NASW *Code of Ethics* and pertinent state law concerning the disclosure of confidential information, particularly whether there is evidence of imminent, serious, and foreseeable harm. A key consideration in this case is that the charges against the teenager are pending; she has not been adjudicated, and the social worker may not know whether or to what extent the evidence against the teenager is compelling.

In addition to circumstances involving clients who appear to pose a threat to third parties, social workers must be familiar with various other guidelines concerning the release of confidential information. For example, social workers also need to know about the proper management of confidential information related to alcohol and substance abuse treatment. In case 2.24, the social worker was approached by a police detective, who asked the social worker for confidential information about a man who had been a guest at the homeless shelter. Strict federal regulations (42 C.F.R. §2-1 ff.[1987]) limit social workers' disclosure of confidential information. These regulations broadly protect the confidentiality of records with respect to the identity, diagnosis, prognosis, or treatment of clients in connection with any program or activity relating to substance abuse education, prevention, training, treatment, rehabilitation, or research that is conducted, regulated, or directly or indirectly assisted by any federal department or agency. Disclosures are permitted with the written, informed consent of the client; to medical personnel in emergencies; for research, evaluation, and audits; and by court order for good cause. Social workers employed by a homeless shelter would be obligated to adhere to these strict criteria if these legal conditions are met.

Social workers employed in school settings must be familiar with the Family Educational Rights and Privacy Act (FERPA, also known as Buckley – 20 U.S.C. § 1232g [1974, as amended]; 34 C.F.R. Part 99 [1974]). This federal law protects the privacy of student education records and applies to all schools that receive money from the U.S. Department of Education. FERPA gives parents certain rights with respect to their children's education records. For example, parents or eligible students have the right to inspect and review the student's education records maintained by the school. Generally, schools must have written permission from the parent or eligible student to release any information from a student's education record. However, FERPA allows schools to disclose those records, without consent, to certain parties and under specific conditions (for example, to comply with a judicial order or lawfully issued subpoenaed, in cases of health and safety emergencies).

Social workers sometimes receive requests for confidential information about former clients who have died. Surviving family members of a client who committed suicide may seek information to help them understand and cope with their loss, or social workers may be subpoenaed in a legal matter involving a dispute among family members concerning the former client's will. A newspaper reporter or law enforcement official may request information about a deceased client who was somehow involved in a serious crime, or an Internal Revenue Service official may ask for information about a deceased client's lifestyle.

In short, clients' confidentiality rights do not end in death; thus social workers must take careful steps to protect the confidentiality of deceased clients. As the NASW *Code of Ethics* states, "Social workers should protect the confidentiality of deceased clients" (standard 1.07[r]). Practitioners should not disclose confidential information unless they have obtained proper legal authorization to do so (for example, in the form of a court order or permission from the legal representative of the deceased client's estate).

Social workers who provide services to children and adolescents sometimes must make difficult decisions about the disclosure of confidential information, as in case 2.25, where the father of a minor client asked the social worker for confidential information about the child's counseling. Often these situations occur when minors are engaging in risky behaviors (such as high-risk sexual activity, drug abuse, suicidal gestures) or threaten harm to others.

State laws and regulations vary with respect to social workers' obligations in these situations. Social workers should consult local statutes, regulations, and officials to determine the extent to which they are obligated to disclose confidential information to parents and guardians, even without the minor client's consent; permitted—but not obligated—to disclose confidential information to parents or guardians without the minor client's consent; and not permitted to disclose confidential information to parents or guardians without the minor client's consent.

Social workers who provide services to families, couples, or groups sometimes encounter difficult ethical dilemmas related to confidentiality. For example, members of a family, couple, or group may not respect other clients' confidentiality or will expect the social worker to "keep secrets" from other family, couple, or group members. There is some difference of opinion among social workers with respect to whether individual family members should be able to share information confidentially with assurance that it will not be shared with other family members in the counseling context.

Many social workers will not provide individual counseling to clients they are seeing in family, couples, or marital therapy because this can introduce clinical complexity. These social workers explain to clients at the beginning of the therapeutic relationship that the family or couple is the client and they will not meet with the participants individually; any participant who wants individual counseling can ask for a referral to another practitioner. This may be accompanied by a statement that the social worker does not keep secrets and that it is important for the participants to be able to raise issues openly in the context of the counseling.

In contrast, some practitioners are willing to meet individually with participants in family, couples, or group counseling sessions if all the participants agree at the beginning of the counseling that this is acceptable. Social workers who favor this approach typically explain that anyone who is seen individually will be regarded as a separate client with a separate case record and with an individual client's rights to confidentiality. That is, other participants in the family, couples, or group counseling will not have access to the case record involving the individual counseling.

Social workers who provide group counseling typically have a policy that they will not talk individually with any group member about any other group member. This policy enhances trust among group members and avoids any perception of favoritism on the social worker's part or complex alliances between the social worker and certain individual clients. There may be an occasional exception to this policy—for example, when a group counseling client also is receiving individual counseling from the social worker facilitating the group and the client feels the need to talk to the social worker about how to handle some troubling interpersonal dynamics in the group. As a routine matter, social workers should explain to group counseling participants how they handle such situations; under what, if any, circumstances other group members would be discussed in individual counseling sessions; and the extent to which this information would be considered confidential.

Social workers sometimes receive requests for confidential information from third parties who have some interest in clients' circumstances. A parent may ask for information about her or his child, as in case 2.25, or an insurance representative, journalist, or police official may request confidential details. Social workers need to handle these requests carefully, avoiding disclosure without written authorization by the client or other legitimate party. When clients authorize disclosure, or a judge orders disclosure, social workers should always limit the disclosure as much as possible. As the NASW *Code of Ethics* states: "In all instances, social workers should disclose the least amount of confidential information necessary to achieve the desired purpose; only information that is directly relevant to the purpose for which the disclosure is made should be revealed" (standard 1.07[c]).

Many social workers are asked to disclose confidential information during legal proceedings, such as malpractice or personal injury lawsuits, divorce cases, termination-of-parental-rights proceedings, and criminal court hearings. Social workers are obligated to protect clients' confidentiality during such legal proceedings to the extent permitted by law. To do so, they need to understand the concepts of privileged communication and subpoena. The concept of privilege concerns the admissibility of information during legal proceedings, especially the extent to which courts may compel disclosure of confidential information. Many states have laws granting the right of privileged communication to social workers' clients during legal proceedings. Also, in a landmark case, *Jaffe v. Redmond* (1996), the U.S. Supreme Court ruled that clinical social workers and their clients have the right of privileged communication in federal courts. Social workers who receive a subpoena to produce confidential records or testify about confidential matters should attempt to protect clients' confidentiality to the greatest extent possible.

A wide range of modern technological innovations have enabled social workers to transmit confidential information quickly and efficiently. Social workers now commonly take advantage of electronic transmission via fax, e-mail, Web site chat room, and text messaging. Each of these appealing tools carries some risk, particularly related to the unauthorized or inappropriate disclosure of confidential information. Faxed documents can expose sensitive information, particularly when they linger in the receiving fax machine's tray for extended periods of time. E-mail communications and text messages can be misdirected.

Social workers who transfer a case record or other confidential material to another agency or colleague should take steps to protect the confidentiality of the information. As in case 2.26—where the social worker had important confidential information from her previous job concerning the potential risk posed by an applicant for a group home bed in the practitioner's current agency—social workers need to protect confidential information that might be shared between agencies and practitioners. Without consent or a court order, or compelling evidence of an imminent, serious, or foreseeable risk to clients or others, social workers should not transfer confidential information from one setting to another.

55

Social workers need to prepare for the possibility that they may not be able to continue working with clients because of disability, illness, employment termination, or death. Practitioners should develop procedures to ensure continuity of service and to protect clients' confidential records. This may include arranging for colleagues to assume at least initial responsibility for their clients if the social worker is unable to continue practicing. Such steps may include oral or written agreements with colleagues or stipulations that appear in a plan that a social worker develops with the assistance of a lawyer (for example, designating a personal representative who will manage the social worker's professional affairs). Many experts recommend that social workers prepare a will that includes plans for the transfer or disposition of cases if the practitioner dies or becomes incapacitated.

Occasionally social workers have clients who do not pay their bills for service in a timely fashion. It is reasonable for social workers to contact collection agencies when they encounter serious difficulty with collecting unpaid fees. Before doing so, social workers should make every effort to provide clients with sufficient notice and reasonable payment plans. When social workers find it necessary to retain collection agencies, they should have strict procedures to prevent the inappropriate disclosure of confidential information to collection agency staffers. Social workers may disclose the client's contact information and debt amount, but they should not disclose any confidential clinical details. Many states have strict regulations concerning disclosure of information about clients to collection agencies.

Social workers often consult with colleagues about clients. They may do so to sort through difficult clinical issues and think through intervention options. To protect clients, social workers should obtain clients' consent to consult with colleagues and should share with consultants the least amount of confidential information necessary to achieve the purposes of the consultation.

Special confidentiality challenges arise when social workers supervise volunteers in social service agencies. Social workers should take steps to ensure that volunteers receive comprehensive training about the management of confidential information and have access only to the confidential information that is necessary to carry out their duties; that is, volunteers should have access to confidential information only on a "need-to-know" basis. Many agencies ask volunteers to sign formal confidentiality agreements that spell out their duties and responsibilities.

Social workers who teach students or train practitioners should be careful about their presentation of confidential material, particularly during case discussions. In such instances social workers should not disclose any identifying information without clients' informed consent. Clients' names should not be mentioned, and presenters should disguise or alter case-related details to ensure anonymity. Any written case material should be similarly disguised.

Social workers who present audio- or video-recorded material should also take careful steps to protect clients. Such material should not be presented unless clients have provided informed consent to the taping itself and to the presentation of the material. With video records it may be possible to protect client confidentiality by recording clients from an angle that limits their visibility or by blurring their distinguishing facial or other characteristics.

Classroom educators should ensure that their students understand their obligation to protect client confidentiality when case material is incorporated into written assignments. Educators should discuss with students various ways in which they can disguise case material and avoid disclosing identifying information.

Social workers would do well to understand their duty to respond to media requests skillfully. Newspaper, television, radio, and Web site reporters often seek out social workers for information pertaining to newsworthy cases. Social workers who are approached by members of the media must protect their clients' confidentiality. Social workers may comment generally about pertinent issues but should do so in a way that does not violate clients' rights.

NASW *Code of Ethics* standards: Commitment to Clients (1.01); Self-Determination (1.02); Informed Consent (1.03); Privacy and Confidentiality (1.07 and 2.02); Consultation (2.05); Evaluation and Research (5.02)

Discussion Questions

1. You are a clinical social worker at a community mental health center. Your client is a 12-year-old boy who was brought to you for counseling by his mother. The boy's mother and father are in the midst of a bitter divorce and custody dispute. One day the boy's father calls you on the telephone and says he would like to know what his son has been saying about him in counseling sessions. The father also wants you to mail him a copy of your clinical notes. How would you respond to the father? What are the important privacy and confidentiality issues?

2. You are a case manager at a family services agency. The agency's assistant director asks you to design a comprehensive in-service training session on privacy and confidentiality. The training session will be for all agency staff, including clinicians, case managers, supervisors, administrators, and office staff. What topics would you address in your presentation?

3. You provide counseling services to men and women who are members of a support group for people who struggle with chronic and persistent mental illness. During one group session a man becomes agitated as he talks about an argument he had with his partner. The man blurts out, "I can't believe she called the cops on me again. This time she went too far. She's going to pay for this." You are concerned about the man's partner's safety. Would you consider disclosing the man's confidential comment without his permission? What confidentiality guidelines would you consider? What steps would you take to make this ethical decision?

4. You are a social worker at a high school. One of your students, a 16-year-old girl, disclosed to you that she is pregnant. She is distraught and would like information about her options. The girl says that she is thinking about terminating the pregnancy but does not give you permission to disclose the pregnancy to her parents. Does the student have the right to confidentiality, or do you have a duty to disclose this information to her parents? How would you respond if the student asked you to help her make plans to terminate her pregnancy?

Access to Records

CASE 2.27. A social worker in private practice provided counseling to a 37-year-old woman who sought help to resolve long-standing conflict with her husband. The client had filed for divorce and sought sole custody of the couple's children; she asked the social worker to testify on her behalf. The client assumed that the social worker would provide supportive testimony. However, the social worker's clinical notes included some comments about the client's emotional instability and conflict in her relationship with her children.

The client asked the social worker for a copy of her clinical notes so that she could share them with her lawyer. The social worker was concerned that her client would be very upset and angry when she saw the notes. The social worker wondered whether she should share her notes with her client.

CASE 2.28. A social worker in a psychiatric hospital provided clinical services to a 52-year-old man who was diagnosed with schizophrenia. The client occasionally reported that he hears voices and sometimes struggles with paranoia. His neuroleptic medication was effective most of the time. Ordinarily the man cooperated and got along well with the social worker, although sometimes the man believed that the social worker is the devil.

At the end of one clinical appointment, the man told the social worker that he had a nightmare about him and thinks the social worker has been writing "bad" things about him in his notes. The client asked the social worker to show him his clinical notes. The social worker worried that reading the clinical notes might upset the client and exacerbate his symptoms.

Discussion

Earlier in social work's history, many social workers believed that their clinical records belonged to them and that they should limit clients' access to them. Over time, professionals' opinions on this issue have changed significantly. More recently, social workers have come to appreciate why clients may need or want to see their records and that such disclosure can indeed have therapeutic value if handled sensitively and skillfully.

Many agencies and private practitioners have developed policies concerning clients' access to records. Clients may be allowed to have photocopied portions of the record, for instance, or may examine the record while in the presence of a professional staff person. Such policies often spell out the circumstances in which clients may be denied access to their record, such as when the social worker has reason to believe that the client would be harmed emotionally. In these instances an alternative is to release the information to the client's legal representative. Of course, social workers must be careful not to share the contents of a client's case record with family members, significant others, or guardians without proper consent or legal authorization.

When clients are competent, the presumption is that they have the right to examine their own record. In case 2.27, for example, there does not appear to be any justification for withholding the record from the client. Understandably, the social worker was concerned that the client may become upset and angry when she sees the notes, which include some critical comments about the client. The social worker would have to deal with the possible clinical fallout that may result and would probably learn a painful lesson in the process about why it is important to record clinical notes assuming that someday clients and third parties may review the notes. In actuality, this may not happen often, but social workers are wise to record their notes in a way that anticipates client and third-party review.

The circumstances in case 2.28 raise very different issues. In this instance the social worker had justifiable concerns about the client's ability to understand and process the clinical notes. With good reason, the social worker was concerned that the client may misunderstand some of the notes and suffer emotionally as a result. Inevitably these sorts of circumstances concern clients' competence to consent, in this instance to their right to access their own records. As discussed earlier, social workers who deliver services to people with diminished capacity should attempt to obtain informed consent from an individual who is authorized to act on the client's behalf. This may be a relative, guardian, or some other individual who has legal authority to provide consent. Social workers must remember that, although clients may lack the capacity to provide informed consent (because of a permanent disability or temporary incapacity), clients retain the right to receive information about themselves, which may be contained in their records, consistent with their level of understanding and comprehension.

NASW *CODE OF ETHICS* STANDARDS: Commitment to Clients (1.01); Self-Determination (1.02); Informed Consent (1.03); Privacy and Confidentiality (1.07); Access to Records (1.08); Consultation (2.05)

DISCUSSION QUESTIONS

1. One of your clients has been difficult to manage. He has missed many appointments and, when he meets with you, is often argumentative. After the client misses a third scheduled appointment in a row, you inform him—on the basis of your supervisor's recommendation—that you would no longer be able to schedule appointments. You explain to the client that you will be terminating services and will help him locate another provider.

   The client becomes enraged and threatens to sue you and the agency for abandoning him. He insists that you provide him with a photocopy of his clinical record. How would you respond?

2. You are counseling a 12-year-old child whose parents are divorcing. The parents are in the middle of a bitter custody dispute. You have provided counseling primarily to the child. However, on six occasions you also counseled his father, who asked you for individual sessions to help him address his increasing anxiety surrounding the divorce and the apparent impact on his child. Furthermore, on two occasions you met with both the mother and father to discuss parenting issues.

The mother's lawyer calls your office and insists that you mail her a copy of your clinical record. You realize that the lawyer is interested in seeing whether your clinical record contains any information that might be used to discredit the father (for example, negative or critical comments about the father's emotional state or parenting ability) and bolster the mother's legal position in the divorce and custody dispute. How would you respond to the attorney's request for a copy of your clinical record?

Sexual Relationships

CASE 2.29. A social worker at an outpatient mental health clinic provided counseling to a 32-year-old male army veteran who struggled with posttraumatic stress symptoms. At the end of their final clinical session, after about six months of weekly counseling, the client said, "You know, lately I've found myself thinking an awful lot about you, but not about you as my therapist. I mean, I've been having thoughts about how nice it would be to, you know, get involved with you. I feel kind of silly saying this, but I can't seem to stop thinking about you. I really don't want to say goodbye to you."

The social worker responded by saying, "I never imagined that I'd by saying this, but I've been having similar feelings about you. I'm not quite sure what to do about them. You probably know that I could get in trouble in my profession if we get involved. This has never happened to me before."

CASE 2.30. A social worker in a hospice program provided clinical services to a 54-year-old woman who was dying of uterine cancer. During a five-week period the social worker spent considerable time with the woman discussing her life experiences and her feelings of grief and loss. About half of the clinical sessions included one or both of the woman's two closest friends.

Two weeks after the woman's death, the social worker received a telephone call from one of the two friends; the caller explained that the two friends felt the need for some "closure" and plan to get together at her home in a week for a casual dinner and a memorial ceremony. The caller invited the social worker to join them: "During our brief time together, all three of us felt very close to you. You became an intimate part of our lives. It would mean so much to [the other friend of the deceased client] and me if you would join us next week at my home. Both of us feel like you belong there."

The social worker attended the dinner and memorial ceremony. One week later, the friend who initially extended the invitation called the social worker and asked her if she would like to get together again for dinner. The social worker agreed. Before long, the two began to date and eventually moved in together.

Discussion

As discussed in the section on dual and multiple relationships, social workers must be very careful in their efforts to maintain clear boundaries in their relationships with clients and former clients. Clearly this includes avoiding any sexual activities or contact with current clients. Any form of sexual activity or contact with clients is generally considered self-serving and exploitative, regardless of the social worker's motives. Clients who become sexually involved with their social workers are likely to be confused about the nature and purposes of the relationship, and this is likely to harm them.

Sexual misconduct typically has devastating consequences. For victimized clients, common consequences include destroyed self-esteem, destructive dependency, mistrust of the opposite sex (for heterosexual victims), distrust of therapists, difficulty in subsequent intimate relationships, impaired sexual relationships, guilt, self-blame, suicidal ideation, substance abuse, loss of confidence, cognitive dysfunction, increased anxiety, identity disturbances, sexual confusion, mood lability, suppressed rage, depression, psychosomatic disorders, and feelings of anger, rejection, isolation, and abandonment.

Social workers generally agree that practitioners also should not enter into sexual relationships with former clients. The social workers in cases 2.29 and 2.30 need to be mindful of evolving ethical and legal standards concerning practitioners' sexual relationships with former clients. In fact, many states now prohibit, by statute or regulation, sexual relationships with former clients.

Contemporary social workers have a keen understanding of potential harm to social workers' former clients. First, it is not unusual for former clients, such as the client in case 2.29, to face challenging issues in their lives after the formal termination of the professional–client relationship. New emotional issues, relationship problems, or developmental crisis may emerge, and former clients may find it useful to contact the social worker for assistance. The social worker's familiarity with the client's circumstances and the established relationship between the social worker and the client may be especially helpful in such cases; it may be burdensome to the client to begin anew with another mental health professional. Clearly, however, a social worker and a former client who have entered into a sexual relationship could have difficulty resuming an effective professional–client relationship. Social workers and former clients who enter into sexual relationships after the termination of their professional–client relationship essentially forfeit resuming that relationship, and this may not be in the client's best interest.

Second, former clients may encounter less challenging new issues or problems in their lives and still may find it helpful to speculate on their own about what their former social worker would have said about the matter. The former client may not feel the need to resume a formal relationship with the social worker; however, the client might find it helpful merely to reflect on the social worker's perspective. A sexual relationship between the social worker and the former client presumably would interfere with the former client's ability to draw on what he or she has learned from the social worker's professional experience, given the shift from a professional to an intimate relationship. Thus, social workers should consider their clients as "clients in perpetuity": once a client, always a client.

NASW *Code of Ethics* standards: Commitment to Clients (1.01); Self-Determination (1.02); Informed Consent (1.03); Conflicts of Interest (1.06); Sexual Relationships (1.09); Physical Contact (1.10); Sexual Harassment (1.11); Consultation (2.05); Unethical Conduct of Colleagues (2.11); Impairment (4.05)

Discussion questions
1. Are there any circumstances under which you think it would be permissible for a social worker to engage in a sexual relationship with a former client? If so, what are they? If not, why not?
2. Some social workers believe that there ought to be exceptions to the prohibition concerning sexual relationships with former clients for social workers who are not clinicians (for example, administrators, policy analysts, community organizers). Do you think the same ethical standards should apply to all social workers, or do you think there ought to be exceptions for social workers who are not clinicians? What criteria would you use to determine whether a social worker is a clinician?

Physical Contact

Case 2.31. A social worker at a group home for adolescent girls provided crisis counseling to a 16-year-old resident who had been sexually abused by her stepfather. The girl was referred to the group home after she was hospitalized following a drug over-dose. One afternoon, the girl became distraught when she learned that her mother was killed in an automobile accident. She asked the social worker if she would "please hold me, hold me, hold me" while the two of them talked about the girl's tragic loss.

CASE 2.32. A social worker in a home health agency provided supportive counsel-ing to patients struggling with chronic illness. One of her clients was a 67-year-old woman who was recovering from a serious stroke. The woman and her family were observant Orthodox Jews.

One afternoon the social worker drove to her client's home for a professional visit. The client's husband opened the front door; the social worker reached out and grabbed the husband's hand to greet him. The client's husband was startled by the social worker's gesture, pulled his hand away from hers, and seemed visibly upset.

Discussion

It is not unusual for social workers to have some kind of modest physical contact with clients, for example, a brief hug at the end of the final professional visit follow-ing a long-term professional–client relationship and a handshake at the very begin-ning of a professional–client relationship. Most practitioners would not find this kind of physical contact objectionable or inappropriate.

Yet, some forms of practitioner–client physical contact, even when they are not explicitly sexual in nature, are more troubling. Social workers must always be careful to distinguish between appropriate and inappropriate physical contact with clients. Some forms of physical contact have the potential to cause clients emotional harm. In general, inappropriate physical contact occurs when the nature of the contact might exacerbate the client's emotional condition. This can be particularly prob-lematic when the client concludes from the physical contact that the relationship extends beyond the formal professional–client relationship. These situations can be problematic because the social worker's conduct has the potential to confuse cli-ents about the nature of the professional–client relationship and introduce complex boundary issues into the relationship. Some forms of touch, especially cradling or caressing clients, are likely to distract both social workers and clients from their therapeutic agenda and thus jeopardize the client's well-being. Also, as in case 2.31, it is possible that physical contact could traumatize a client who associates the con-tact with earlier incidents of molestation. Other than brief contact within a thera-peutic context—such as a quick hug to say good-bye or to comfort a distraught client—physical touch is likely to cause emotional harm and interfere with the professional–client relationship.

Social workers should also be aware that some cultures, ethnic groups, and religious groups have strict norms and rules about physical contact, especially between men and women. Social workers should strive to learn about and be sensitive to these issues. In case 2.32, for example, it would have been helpful for the social worker to know that many Orthodox Jewish men do not shake hands with women in order to limit sensual contact to the marital relationship.

NASW *CODE OF ETHICS* STANDARDS: Commitment to Clients (1.01); Self-Determination (1.02); Informed Consent (1.03); Cultural Competence and Social Diversity (1.05); Conflicts of Interest (1.06); Physical Contact (1.10); Sexual Harassment (1.11); Consultation (2.05); Unethical Conduct of Colleagues (2.11); Impairment (4.05)

DISCUSSION QUESTIONS

1. You have several part-time social work jobs in various settings: a private middle and high school, a pediatric psychiatric hospital, and a nursing home. What forms of physical contact would be appropriate in these settings? What forms of physical contact would not be appropriate?

2. Your supervisor at the pediatric psychiatric hospital has asked you to develop a policy concerning physical contact with clients. What criteria would you include in the policy to distinguish between appropriate and inappropriate physical contact?

Payment for Services

CASE 2.33. A social worker in private practice provided counseling services to a 27-year-old man who had been sexually abused as a child. At the time the counseling began, the client worked for a large manufacturing company. The counseling was very productive; the client reported that he is functioning much better and has learned some valuable anxiety-management techniques.

About three months after the counseling began, the client was laid off by his employer. As a result, he no longer had insurance coverage for mental health services. However, the client desperately wanted to continue counseling. He had serious financial problems and was contemplating declaring bankruptcy. The social worker had to decide whether to see the client without payment or for a modest fee.

CASE 2.34. A social worker in private practice provided counseling to a 38-year-old woman who struggled with substance abuse and clinical depression. The client earned her living as an artist and did not have health insurance. She paid for counseling sessions out of pocket.

The client explained to the social worker that she was having financial difficulty and wondered whether the social worker would be willing to select several of the client's art works in exchange for counseling services.

Discussion

Social workers are entitled to fair compensation for the services they render. Social workers who are in independent or private practice set their fees on the basis of various factors, including their level of education, training, professional experience, and the prevailing fees in the local community. In addition, social workers who are preferred providers for insurance companies may accept the companies' fee schedule or negotiate specific reimbursement rates. Some social workers do not accept third-party payment.

The NASW *Code of Ethics* encourages social workers to consider clients' ability to pay when they set fees: "When setting fees, social workers should ensure that the fees are fair, reasonable, and commensurate with the services performed. Consideration should be given to clients' ability to pay" (standard 1.13[a]). Moreover, the code's broad ethical principles encourage social workers "to volunteer some portion of their professional skills with no expectation of significant financial return (pro bono service)" (p. 5). Historically, the social work profession has been concerned about the well-being of low-income and other vulnerable people. Thus, in cases 2.33 and 2.34 it is both appropriate and commendable that the social workers were eager to provide clinical services to their financially strapped clients.

The majority of clients (or their insurance providers) pay fees for social work services, but in a relatively few cases social workers participate in barter arrangements when clients are unable to pay for services and offer goods or services as a substitute. Bartering also occurs in some communities, particularly rural ones, in which there are established norms involving such nonmonetary exchange of goods and services.

One might conclude that barter is not unethical when the parties participate willingly and have no ulterior motives. In reality, however, barter can lead to significant ethical challenges. For example, in case 2.34 the social worker and client would have to agree on the monetary value of the client's artistic works. If the social worker believes the art is not as valuable as does the client, the client might feel wounded emotionally or exploited, and this could complicate their clinical relationship. If a client offered to provide a service, such as car repair or house painting, rather than a tangible good like art work, problems can arise if there is a problem with the quality of the client's technical skill or performance. For example, if the car repair fails or the painted house begins to deteriorate prematurely, negotiating a remedy might introduce tension and discomfort that undermines the clinical relationship.

Social workers should be aware that arriving at a fair market value for some goods and services can be challenging. Some goods and services—such as a bushel of wheat, a car engine replacement, and a new house roof—have widely understood fair market values. However, the fair market value of other goods and services— such as a custom-made quilt, a musical performance, or landscape design—may be harder to quantify.

Some social workers believe that barter is more likely to be acceptable ethically in communities where it is an accepted practice. In some rural communities, for example, professionals—such as doctors, dentists, farmers, and plumbers—may exchange goods for services. Consequently, although the NASW *Code of Ethics* discourages barter, it does not prohibit it categorically. The code states that social workers should avoid bartering and that they should accept goods or services from clients as payments for professional services only in very limited circumstances when certain conditions are met. The social worker in case 2.34 should ask herself a series of questions: First, to what extent are such barter arrangements an accepted practice among professionals in the local community? The widespread use of barter in the local community can strengthen a social worker's belief that barter is appropriate in a particular case. Second, to what extent is barter essential for the provision of services? Is it used mainly because it is the most expedient and convenient form of payment available, or is it used because it is the only feasible way for the client to obtain needed services? As a general rule, barter should be considered only as a last resort when more conventional forms of payment (fee for service, insurance payment) are not feasible and only when barter seems to be essential for the delivery of services. Third, is the barter arrangement negotiated without coercion or exploitation? Social workers should not pressure clients to agree to barter. Clients are in a vulnerable position and may feel pressure to accede to a social worker's barter terms, even when clients believe the terms are unfair. Clients who agree to participate in a barter arrangement must do so freely and willingly, without any direct or indirect coercion from the social worker. Fourth, was the barter arrangement entered into at the client's initiative and with the client's informed consent? To avoid coercing clients or the appearance of any impropriety, social workers should not take the initiative to suggest barter as an option. Such suggestions should come from clients, with their fully informed consent. When barter arrangements seem feasible and ethically appropriate, social workers should explain the nature and terms of the arrangement in clear and understandable language and discuss any risks associated with barter (for example, how the professional–client relationship could be adversely affected, how disputes would be resolved), reasonable alternatives for payment (for example, a reduced installment payment rather than payment in full), the client's right to refuse or withdraw consent, and the time frame covered by the consent.

Social workers must recognize that even when all these conditions have been met, they assume the full burden of demonstrating that bartering will not be detrimental to the client or the professional relationship. Social workers' principal responsibility is to protect clients. Practitioners must always exercise sound judgment when considering the risks associated with barter.

NASW CODE OF ETHICS STANDARDS: Commitment to Clients (1.01); Self-Determination (1.02); Informed Consent (1.03); Conflicts of Interest (1.06); Payment for Services (1.13); Interruption of Services (1.15); Termination of Services (1.16); Consultation (2.05)

DISCUSSION QUESTIONS

1. Many social workers are sensitive to the needs of low-income people and clients with few assets. What is your own personal philosophy with regard to providing services to clients who have difficulty paying for them?

2. Suppose you are a social worker in independent practice. You understand that clients occasionally have difficulty paying for services. Under what circumstances, if any, would you consider bartering with a client? What steps would you take to ensure that clients are protected?

Clients Who Lack Decision-Making Capacity

CASE 2.35. A social worker in a program that provides services to victims of domestic violence worked with a 27-year-old woman who fled her abusive husband. According to the woman, her husband abuses alcohol and, when he is drunk, often becomes physically and verbally assaultive. The woman has sought refuge at the agency's emergency shelter on three separate occasions. The woman struggled with the consequences of a childhood brain injury and had mild cognitive impairment.

Once again the woman appeared on the shelter's doorstep asking for help. After three days, the woman informed the social worker that she spoke to her husband, who promised he would not harm her again. The woman told the social worker that "This time he sounds like he really means it. I do love him; he just gets real mean when he has that liquor in him. I have a feeling this time is different. I'm going to give him another chance."

The social worker had doubts about the woman's judgment, particularly given her somewhat limited cognitive ability. On the basis of her extensive experience in the domestic violence field, the social worker felt strongly that the woman was still at risk and would likely be harmed again by her husband.

CASE 2.36. A social worker at a group home run by a state psychiatric hospital worked with a 62-year-old man who had schizophrenia. At times the man functioned well; at other times the man struggled with hallucinations and delusions.

The man was diagnosed with pancreatic cancer. His physician, a seasoned oncologist, recommended an aggressive treatment strategy including surgery, radiation, and chemotherapy. The physician explained the options to the man, who adamantly rejected the recommendations. The man said, "I don't believe in those things. I think God has decided what should happen to me, and that's that."

CASE 2.37. A social worker at a family service agency provided counseling to a 16-year-old girl who was experiencing significant emotional turmoil. The girl's parents were divorcing. She was truant from school occasionally, hanging out with teenagers who abuse drugs and alcohol, and becoming more and more defiant at home.

During one counseling session the girl told the social worker that she just found out that she is six weeks pregnant. The girl said that she wants to terminate the pregnancy but refused to give permission to the social worker to share this news with her parents. The girl explained that she is having so much conflict with her parents that she cannot possible "add this fuel to the fire." The girl said she wanted to make this decision herself.

Discussion

Social workers sometimes provide services to clients who lack the capacity to make informed decisions as a result of mental illness, brain injury, age, medication, substance abuse, or some other kind of disability. Ordinarily, a person is considered incompetent when, because of mental illness, age, cognitive disability, or substance abuse she or he is incapable of either managing her or his property or caring for herself or himself.

To protect such clients, social workers should be knowledgeable about their legal rights. In general, adults in the United States are presumed to be legally competent and entitled to make all decisions for themselves. People can be deprived of this right only if they have been determined to be incompetent by a court that considers evidence concerning mental or physical impairment, or if there is a law that denies certain individuals (for example, minors) the right to consent. It is possible that a person is considered to have a mental illness, a developmental disability, or an addiction, for example, but is competent to make decisions, manage money, and care for herself or himself; that is, impairment or disability does not, by itself, imply incompetence.

Social workers who provide services to clients who lack the capacity to make informed decisions should be knowledgeable about these clients' rights in a number of key areas. Social workers should protect clients' interests by seeking informed consent on a client's behalf, when necessary, from an appropriate third party (proxy or substituted judgment). This person usually is a spouse, partner, or other relative who is likely to act in the client's best interests or who has been appointed as the client's legal guardian. To the extent possible, a social worker should explain to such a client, in a manner consistent with the client's level of understanding, what services are being provided, what options are available, and what decisions are being made. This approach is certainly relevant in case 2.36, where the client's understanding of the ramifications of his illness and treatment options may be somewhat limited. This approach may not be possible with some clients (for example, clients with profound mental disability or serious brain injury), but it is possible with many (for example, certain clients with moderate mental disability or who are recovering from a serious drug overdose).

Social workers should also be aware that many states now require that judicial decisions concerning an individual's incompetence should focus narrowly on specific issues or circumstances rather than take the form of a broad determination that an individual is incompetent for any and all purposes. Thus, a client may be considered incompetent to make sound decisions about handling complex financial matters yet competent to make a decision about health care or housing options. A court might then appoint a guardian to handle only the client's financial matters; the guardian would not have the authority to determine whether the client treats a chronic health care condition aggressively or where the client will live. Many states recognize the concept of "least restrictive alternative" as a guiding principle, which states that a person considered incompetent should lose only those rights that he or she cannot properly exercise.

Generally speaking, competent adults have a right to refuse medical treatment. When an individual is incompetent, a court may appoint a legal guardian to make a decision on that individual's behalf. A court may also use a substituted judgment test by which it attempts to determine what the client would want. This subjective test contrasts with an objective test by which the court attempts to determine what a "reasonable person" would want. Some courts have recognized an incompetent individual's prior expression of wishes and desires concerning medical treatment, even when such wishes and desires were not documented in writing, as in a living will.

Although in most cases minor children are not considered competent to consent to their own medical treatment, exceptions do exist. In many states minor children are permitted to consent to medical treatment in cases of genuine emergency or if they want assistance with birth control or treatment for substance abuse or a sexually transmitted disease. Some states also permit minors who want to terminate a pregnancy to seek the court's permission—in lieu of parental notification—when there is evidence that the minor would be at risk of physical or emotional abuse if parents were informed of the pregnancy and the teenager's wish to terminate it (this is known as judicial bypass). However, in the absence of compelling evidence that the minor would be at risk, state law may require parental notification. These are relevant considerations in case 2.37.

Cases such as 2.35—where clients appear to be sufficiently, albeit perhaps minimally, competent to make decisions—are particularly challenging for social workers, especially when clients' judgment may place them in harm's way. In such instances social workers certainly have a duty to ensure that clients understand the information pertaining to their decision, including possible positive and negative consequences. In the final analysis, however, social workers should not coerce clients who satisfy widely respected competency criteria.

NASW *CODE OF ETHICS* STANDARDS: Commitment to Clients (1.01); Self-Determination (1.02); Informed Consent (1.03); Clients Who Lack Decision-Making Capacity (1.14); Termination of Services (1.16); Consultation (2.05)

DISCUSSION QUESTIONS:
1. You are a social worker in a residential substance abuse treatment program. You are working with a client who has been addicted to heroin for 17 years and whose judgment is very questionable. The client has attempted suicide

and been arrested several times. Clearly he needs a great deal of help. Four weeks after his admission to the six-month program, the client tells you that he has decided to sign himself out. How would you respond?

2. You are a social worker in a pediatric hospital. One of the patients with whom you are working is a 16-year-old girl who has been diagnosed with a form of cancer that is life threatening. You know from speaking with her and reading her medical history that the girl was physically and sexually abused by her uncle, with whom she lived for several years. The girl tells you that her life "has been miserable" and she has decided to refuse medical treatment. "I just want to die," she says. How would you respond? Do you think the girl has a right to refuse medical care?

Termination of Services

CASE 2.38. A social worker at a community mental health center provided counseling services to a 47-year-old man who was diagnosed with major clinical depression. The man had difficulty holding jobs and maintaining relationships with women. During a four-month period, the man missed six of 15 scheduled appointments. On two of these occasions the man canceled his appointment in the morning of the scheduled appointment; on four occasions the man missed his appointment and did not telephone the office ahead of time. Whenever the social worker raised this issue, the man promised he would "do better."

The social worker's supervisor instructed the social worker to notify the man that the agency could no longer treat him as a client because of the pattern of missed appointments. The social worker shared her supervisor's concerns about the missed appointment but was also concerned about the client's emotional vulnerability.

CASE 2.39. A social worker in private practice provided counseling to a 32-year-old woman who struggled with an eating disorder. The client had been sexually abused as a child and since her high school years had been treated for anorexia nervosa.

The client chose to pay the social worker for the counseling sessions rather than submit the social worker's bill to the insurance carrier provided through the client's employment. The client told the social worker that she was concerned about her privacy and preferred to pay for the counseling herself.

The client owed the social worker nearly $1,200. Each time the social worker raised the issue of the unpaid bill, the client apologized and promised the social worker that she would pay a significant amount "soon." The social worker sensed that the client was becoming increasingly ambivalent about counseling and considered terminating the client because of the client's unwillingness to address the unpaid bill.

CASE 2.40. A social worker was employed by a family services agency and provided counseling services to individual clients, couples, and families. After working at the agency for approximately eight years, the social worker decided to resign his position and develop a private practice. The social worker met with the agency's executive director and shared his plans with her. The executive director thanked the social worker, wished him well, and reminded him that he would not be permitted to "take" any of his agency-based clients with him to his new private practice.

Discussion

Social workers terminate services to clients for various reasons. In some instances social workers and their clients agree in advance to work together for a specific period of time; an insurer's coverage may influence this decision. In other instances social workers and clients mutually agree to part ways, either because they are satisfied with the client's progress, the social worker concludes that she or he is not sufficiently helpful, or the client is not satisfied with the progress she or he is making. On occasion the professional–client relationship may end because the client does not or is not able to pay for services or does not comply with a social worker's or agency's policies.

In general, social workers must terminate services when they are no longer required or no longer serve the client's needs or interests. If, in the social worker's judgment, a client has accomplished what he or she set out to achieve, the social worker has a responsibility to talk with the client about terminating the professional–client relationship.

Ethical challenges arise when social workers do not terminate services to and relationships with clients even though the services are no longer needed or no longer serve the clients' needs and interests. This might occur when an unscrupulous social worker who is concerned about his or her income discourages a client from terminating or fails to raise the subject because the social worker wishes to maintain his or her revenue stream. This might also occur when a social worker continues to work with a client for the practitioner's own emotional needs, even though continued services are not warranted. A social worker may find working with a particular client to be especially satisfying and may, perhaps unwittingly, encourage the client's dependency.

Social workers also need to be concerned about terminating services prematurely and not being available when clients need assistance. As noted in cases 2.38 and 2.39, on occasion social workers consider terminating services to clients who miss an inordinate number of appointments, do not pay their bills, or are otherwise "difficult." It is certainly understandable that social workers would be tempted to terminate services in these situations. However, social workers who terminate services to clients who are still in need of assistance or who are not available when needed (for example, when practitioners go on vacation or resign their position) risk allegations of abandonment. *Abandonment* is a legal concept that pertains to instances when a professional is not available to a client when needed. Once a social worker begins to provide services to a client, she or he incurs a legal and ethical responsibility to continue those services or properly refer a client to an alternative services provider.

Social workers should always take careful steps to avoid abandoning clients, such as consulting with colleagues and supervisors about a decision to terminate services and possible alternatives (including ways to remedy the problem and address the social worker's concerns); give as much advance warning as possible to clients who will be terminated; and provide clients with appropriate referrals if social workers are not available or if the client would benefit from consulting with other professionals.

When clients are unwilling or unable to pay an overdue balance for professional services, as in case 2.39, social workers should first discuss with such clients the reasons for nonpayment and take reasonable steps to help clients meet their financial obligations without terminating services (for example, a reasonable payment plan or a reduced fee).

If attempts to address a client's reasons for nonpayment of an overdue balance fail, the social worker may terminate services, but only if the social worker is confident that the client does not pose a danger to himself or herself or others, and if the social worker has discussed with the client the possible clinical and other consequences of the nonpayment and termination of services.

There may be legitimate reasons why social workers might terminate services to clients who still need some form of assistance. Examples include planned retirement, resignation to assume a new position, evidence that clients are not making appropriate progress or cooperating with an intervention plan, lack of expertise to assist clients with their specific needs, being threatened or sued by clients, and clients' failure to pay an overdue balance. Social workers who anticipate the termination or interruption of services to clients for such reasons should work with them to develop a plan to address their needs.

Special ethical challenges arise when social workers decide to leave an employment setting to pursue a new professional challenge, as in case 2.40. Social workers who leave an employment setting should be sure to terminate services properly to avoid abandoning clients. Social workers should always review with clients all appropriate options for the continuation of services. Clients may decide to terminate services if they conclude that their needs have been met. Some clients may choose to continue receiving services in the social worker's current employment setting. In such instances the social worker and the client should work together to identify another professional in the agency with whom the client would feel comfortable working. The social worker would then consult with this colleague to ensure a smooth transfer. Furthermore, some clients may choose to obtain services from another agency or a private provider, and the social worker can facilitate this referral and transition. Finally, when feasible, clients may decide to continue working with the current social worker in her or his new employment setting. Clients of the social worker in case 2.40 certainly have the right to continue with him if they so wish; ethically, the agency director should not prohibit options that best meet clients' needs.

Social workers who inform clients that they may choose to continue working with them in the practitioners' new employment setting must be very careful to ensure that the clients are fully aware that this is merely an option. Social workers should never coerce or pressure clients to follow them to their new employment setting; this would clearly constitute a conflict of interest.

NASW *Code of Ethics* standards: Commitment to Clients (1.01); Self-Determination (1.02); Informed Consent (1.03); Conflicts of Interest (1.06); Interruption of Services (1.15); Termination of Services (1.16); Consultation (2.05); Referral for Services (2.06); Client Transfer (3.06); Commitments to Employers (3.09)

Discussion questions

1. You are a social worker in independent practice. One of your clients, who struggles with bipolar disorder and cocaine addiction, cancels or misses appointments frequently. You have done your best to help the client resolve this problem, but the pattern continues. The client begs you to give him "another chance" and pleads with you to continue counseling him. What would you do?

2. A long-term client of yours, who is in the midst of a bitter divorce and custody dispute, has not paid you for your counseling services for nearly five months. She now owes you around $1,700. What steps would you take

to address this issue? How would you handle the client's request for you to continue providing her with clinical services?

3. You have been employed at a community mental health center for more than seven years. A friend and colleague of yours invites you to join her group private practice. After giving the offer considerable thought, you decide to leave the mental health center and join the group practice. What steps would you take to terminate properly with your clients at the agency?

chapter three

Ethical Responsibilities to Colleagues

Social workers sometimes encounter challenging ethical dilemmas involving their relationships with colleagues. These dilemmas may involve work-site colleagues or professional colleagues in the local or national community. Complex situations can arise involving management of confidential information; interdisciplinary collaboration; disputes with colleagues; consultation; referral for services; boundary issues with colleagues; collegial impairment; and incompetence and unethical conduct of colleagues.

Interdisciplinary Collaboration

CASE 3.1. A social worker who worked on the oncology unit of a large hospital met weekly with an interdisciplinary team to review the status of patients. The team included the social worker, a nursing supervisor, an oncologist, and various allied health professionals (such as an occupational and physical therapist). During one meeting the team discussed the prognosis of a 69-year-old woman who was recently diagnosed with a malignant brain tumor and who was sedated following surgery. The nurse reported that the woman's daughter had asked that the hospital staffers be vague about the patient's grim prognosis when they speak with her mother when she becomes alert. The daughter had explained to the nurse that her mother is very fragile emotionally and "can't possibly handle this kind of information—it will push her over the edge."

The team members discussed how much information they ought to share with the patient. The nurse asserted that in light of the patient's psychiatric history, hospital staffers should be vague about her medical condition and prognosis. However, the social worker felt strongly that the woman had a right to truthful information and that the staffers' challenge was to find a humane, skilled way to communicate the medical details and offer emotional support.

CASE 3.2. A school social worker provided services to a 12-year-old boy. The student was not doing well academically and was isolated socially. The boy's mother told the social worker that the boy seemed to be struggling with sexual orientation issues. The mother asked the social worker to keep this information confidential.

One week later the school's principal stopped by the social worker's office and mentioned that she had received a complaint from another student that the social worker's client had harassed the other student. The principal wanted to know "what's going on" with the social worker's client and asked to see the social worker's notes. The social worker explained to the principal that she is not permitted to disclose confidential information without the mother's consent. The principal insisted that the social worker share whatever relevant information she had about her client.

Discussion

Many social workers are members of interdisciplinary teams, particularly in settings such as hospitals, schools, community mental health centers, the military, substance abuse treatment programs, and correctional facilities. In these settings social workers often collaborate with colleagues from other professions and disciplines to plan, deliver, coordinate, administer, and evaluate social services.

Social workers certainly appreciate the value of interdisciplinary collaboration. Bringing together multiple and diverse perspectives can enrich professionals' ability to serve clients. Discussion and constructive debate among professionals from different fields about the advantages and disadvantages of different intervention approaches can provide useful checks and balances.

As in cases 3.1 and 3.2, it is always possible that professionals will view ethical issues through different, sometimes conflicting, lenses. Colleagues from various professions and disciplines may have different perspectives on the importance of truth telling, privacy and confidentiality, informed consent, and so on. The different professions' norms regarding these issues have evolved over the years, sometimes divergently.

Social workers, like all other professionals, have a responsibility to assert opinions that are rooted in the profession's values and ethical standards. The social worker in case 3.1 would assert social work's traditional commitment to clients' right to know the truth, consistent with their level of understanding and ability to process the information. The social worker in case 3.2 would inform the school principal, as diplomatically as possible, that the social work profession's ethical standards are strict regarding client confidentiality. Social workers' colleagues in other professions may agree or disagree with these views on the basis of the ethical norms in their respective professions. In these challenging circumstances, social workers should be certain to share their unique perspectives and diplomatically assert their relevance. Some settings, such as hospitals, offer formal mechanisms for interdisciplinary dialogue around ethical issues. For example, most hospitals, and many other health care settings, sponsor ethics committees that provide staffers with a forum to discuss these issues. However, in other social service settings—such as schools, child welfare agencies, group homes, and correctional facilities—it is unlikely that a formal ethics committee exists. Social workers may need to take steps to ensure that these key ethics discussions take place in the context of team meetings, staff meetings, and so on.

Disagreements sometimes occur among members of an interdisciplinary team, as in cases 3.1 and 3.2. In many cases these disagreements can be resolved through discussion and skillful management of group dynamics. Occasionally, however, these disagreements are not easily resolved. Social workers sometimes may feel obligated to take a stand on an ethical issue that is contrary to the views of other team members. Social workers who are unable to resolve disagreement among team members about an important ethical issue should try to find alternatives to address their concerns. This may require involving individuals in positions of authority who may be able to resolve the disagreements constructively. If this is not possible, social workers who are convinced that an interdisciplinary team is not handling an ethical matter responsibly have an obligation to address it through other channels.

NASW *Code of Ethics* standards: Commitment to Clients (1.01); Self-Determination (1.02); Informed Consent (1.03); Privacy and Confidentiality (1.07); Respect (2.01); Interdisciplinary Collaboration (2.03); Consultation (2.05); Commitments to Employers (3.09)

Discussion questions

1. You are a social worker at a community action program that provides a range of social services to low-income people, including housing assistance, emergency food, crisis intervention and energy assistance. One of your colleagues, who is not a social worker, learned from a client that two years earlier he robbed a convenience store during a time in his life when he was addicted to heroin. The crime remains unsolved; the man was never arrested

for the robbery. The man has since been in intensive substance abuse treatment and is coping well.

At a staff meeting, your colleague, who does not have a college degree or formal professional education, states that in his opinion the agency has an obligation to report the man to the local police. You believe that the agency has an obligation to protect the man's privacy and that the agency would violate his rights if staffers notified the police. How would you approach these issues in the team meeting?

2. You are employed as a social worker at a senior center that provides a day-treatment program. Many of the program's clients struggle with dementia and other forms of cognitive impairment. At a staff meeting you and your colleagues discuss the challenges faced by a client, an 84-year-old man, who has been diagnosed with moderate cognitive impairment; at times the man is verbally combative and noncompliant. One of your colleagues, a nurse, tells the team that they should consult with the man's primary care physician and psychiatrist about his difficulties. Your colleague shows the group a release of information form that she had the man sign earlier that day authorizing the physicians to release confidential information with the agency. On the basis of your extensive contact with the man and your familiarity with his functioning, you doubt that he read or understood the form he signed. You suspect that he simply complied with the nurse's request that he sign the form. How would you handle this situation?

Consultation

CASE 3.3. A social worker in independent practice belonged to a peer consultation group. The social worker and five colleagues met every two weeks to discuss difficult cases and exchange ideas.

At one meeting a colleague, a clinical psychologist, brought up a case involving one of her clients, a young woman who became clinically depressed and suicidal after discovering that her husband was having an extramarital affair. The colleague wanted feedback about complex aspects of her clinical strategy. Although the colleague did not identify her client by name, she shared enough unique identifying information (age, occupation, family circumstances, home community) that the social worker quickly discovered that the woman's husband was the social worker's client. The psychologist was not aware that the social worker was providing counseling services to the woman's husband.

The social worker was shocked to hear graphic and incriminating details about the husband's extramarital affair. The husband had never disclosed this information to the social worker, even though they spent considerable time discussing his marital issues. The social worker felt misled by the husband; she also felt a need to decide whether to inform him of the troubling information she had learned during the peer consultation group discussion and to explore the clinical implications.

Discussion

It is vitally important for social workers to consult with colleagues. Social workers may lack expertise regarding certain issues or may benefit from feedback offered by colleagues who are able to be somewhat more objective about a complicated situation.

When social workers consult with colleagues about clients, they must be sensitive to clients' right to confidentiality. In fact, social workers should inform clients that they may consult with colleagues occasionally. Many social workers provide clients with written notice at the beginning of their work together informing clients that they occasionally consult with colleagues.

Although clients may consent to social workers' use of consultants, they may not be comfortable having their social workers share certain confidential information with the consultants. As a general rule, social workers should share the least amount of information necessary to accomplish the purposes of the consultation. This protects clients' confidentiality, to the greatest extent possible. In case 3.3, for example, the psychologist should have been careful to omit any identifying information during the group consultation. This would have prevented the ethical dilemma faced by the social worker, who inadvertently learned about her client's (the husband's) clinically significant deception. Unfortunately, the psychologist's disclosure put the social worker in a difficult position. If she ignored the clinically relevant details, the quality of the social worker's counseling of the husband could be greatly compromised. The social worker would have to avoid critically relevant clinical information and, as well, may feel some discomfort and resentment that could affect the clinical relationship. On the other hand, if the social worker shares with the husband the fact that she has learned of the husband's deception (assuming that the allegations concerning the husband's extramarital affair are true), the social worker may introduce tension and complexity into the clinical relationship that might undermine the client's trust and ability to make effective use of the counseling. In addition, the social worker's disclosure might create complications in the psychologist's relationship with her client.

81

In important ways, the social worker may be in a no-win situation. A possible compromise is for the social worker to provide an opportunity for the client to acknowledge these issues, if he so wishes, perhaps by saying something along the lines of, "I know this may be difficult to hear, but I feel the need to share with you some information that I recently received, quite by accident. For ethical reasons, I am not able to disclose the source of the information. I hope you understand that. What I heard, and I have no way of knowing whether it's true, is that you've been involved in an extramarital affair. If it is true, that seems to be very relevant to the marital issues we've been discussing. If it's not true, we can simply move on. I just feel obligated to share this with you." The client can then decide whether to admit to the extramarital affair and discuss it or deny the allegations.

NASW *CODE OF ETHICS* STANDARDS: Commitment to Clients (1.01); Informed Consent (1.03); Privacy and Confidentiality (1.07 and 2.02); Consultation (2.05)

DISCUSSION QUESTIONS

1. The ethical dilemma faced by the social worker in case 3.3 generates diverse opinions about the most appropriate response. If you were the social worker in this case, how would you handle the ethical dilemma? Would you keep the information disclosed by the psychologist to yourself, or would you share it with your client, who is the husband of the psychologist's client?
2. What practical steps would you take to prevent the inappropriate disclosure of confidential information during consultation with colleagues?

Referral for Services

CASE 3.4. A school social worker in a small, rural community provided counseling services to a 12-year-old boy who was having considerable difficulty. His teachers reported that he often seemed inattentive, did not complete many assignments, sometimes blurted out inappropriate comments in class, and was ostracized by many classmates. The social worker suspected that the student might have significant untreated developmental issues. She recommended to the school's principal that they arrange for the boy to be assessed by a pediatrician who specializes in developmental and neurological issues.

Coincidentally, the social worker's wife was a developmental pediatrician who specialized in these very issues. She was the only physician in the rural community with this specialized knowledge and skill. The family, which had limited resources, would have to drive about 90 miles if they were to consult with another physician with this knowledge and skill.

The social worker recognized that referring the boy to his wife might be seen as a conflict of interest. However, the social worker wanted to be sensitive to the boy's and his family's immediate needs.

Discussion

Social workers frequently refer clients who require specialized services or expertise to other professionals. Social workers who refer clients to other professionals should always follow certain procedures. It is important for social workers to discuss with clients the reasons for the referral to ensure that everyone agrees that the referral makes sense. Also, assuming that choices are available locally, several possible professionals to whom clients might be referred should be carefully considered and discussed with the client. Providing clients with a choice of new providers enhances their options and avoids any suggestion that the social worker is trying to steer clients to particular practitioners. In addition, social workers who refer clients to other professionals should disclose, with clients' consent, all pertinent information to the new practitioners. Social workers should discuss with clients which information from the case record is relevant and should be shared with the new service provider to enhance the quality of care and protect privacy to the greatest extent possible. Finally, a social worker should follow up with the client once the referral is made to ensure that the client contacted the new provider.

In some instances, as in case 3.4, it may not be possible to provide clients with the names of several professionals who may be able to meet their needs. Furthermore, a social worker who can refer a client to only one practitioner may encounter a conflict of interest. It is possible, for example, that some individuals will assume that the social worker referred the student to his wife, the physician, for self-interested reasons. Because of this possibility, social workers should always seek consultation to avoid any perception of a conflict of interest. Transparency—disclosing that possible conflict of interest—is the most prudent course of action for all concerned. In case 3.4, for instance, the social worker should inform appropriate school administrators of the unusual situation. One possibility is for another school official to assume responsibility for this student and the referral, to remove the social worker from the situation entirely. In a small community, however, this may not be feasible. At the very least, the social worker, the school administrator, or both should explain the unusual circumstances to the family and provide the family with every available choice, including driving to the closest community that offers comparable expertise. The professionals should document the steps they take to minimize the conflict of interest. This approach is consistent with the NASW *Code of Ethics* standards concerning conflicts of interest: "Social workers should be alert to and avoid conflicts of interest that interfere with the exercise of professional discretion and impartial judgment. Social workers should inform clients when a real or potential conflict of interest arises and take reasonable steps to resolve the issue in a manner that makes the clients' interests primary and protects clients' interests to the greatest extent possible" (standard 1.06[a]).

NASW *CODE OF ETHICS* STANDARDS: Commitment to Clients (1.01); Self-Determination (1.02); Conflicts of Interest (1.06); Consultation (2.05); Referral for Services (2.06)

DISCUSSION QUESTIONS

1. You are a social worker in private practice who has a contract with a nearby college to provide clinical assessment services to students experiencing emotional or mental health problems. According to the contract's terms, when students need counseling beyond crisis intervention, you are expected to assess the students' needs and refer them to one of several local psychotherapists who practice in the community. One of the local psychotherapists offered to pay you the equivalent of her customary hourly fee for each referral. What standards in the NASW *Code of Ethics* apply to this situation? What policy do you think the social worker should establish regarding payment for referrals?

2. You are a high school social worker in a small, rural community. You are friends or acquaintances with many of the local mental health professionals. Your sister is the town's only psychiatrist and your wife is one of two psychotherapists who treat adolescent eating disorders. In a typical year you refer at least a dozen students for psychiatric assessments and several students for treatment of eating disorders. What policies and procedures would you establish to avoid conflicts of interest?

Sexual Relationships

CASE 3.5. A social worker moved to a new community and started a job at a large senior center that provides a day program and in-home services. The social worker was supervised by the agency's senior social worker who was responsible for supervising staffers in four sites.

The new employee met with her supervisor weekly. For several weeks they reviewed information for new employees and discussed the social worker's new clients. Following this initial period, the two met to discuss clients' status, clinical challenges, and so on.

At the end of one supervision session, about 10 months after they began working together, the supervisor told the social worker how well she was performing and that the agency administrators were delighted to have her on staff. The supervisor then commented that on a more personal note, he thoroughly enjoys working with the social worker and was going to recommend that she be promoted to a program director at one of the agency's sites. He then told the social worker how much he liked spending time with her and that he would like to "spend even more time with you outside of here."

The social worker was attracted to her supervisor and agreed to have dinner with him. Within several weeks the two were sexually involved.

CASE 3.6. Two social workers who were colleagues in a substance abuse treatment program were asked by the agency director to collaborate to develop a strategic plan for the agency. The project would take about six months and, at its conclusion, would be submitted to the agency's board of directors for approval.

The two social workers spent approximately a day each week working on the strategic plan. Over time they got to know each other well and were attracted to each other. They began to date and became sexually involved.

About two-thirds of the way through their strategic planning project, the agency director promoted one of the social workers to a supervisory position. The agency director was not aware of the social workers' personal, intimate relationship. As part of her new responsibilities, the social work supervisor would be supervising her colleague and sexual partner.

Discussion

In addition to maintaining clear boundaries in their relationships with clients, social workers must maintain clear boundaries in their relationships with colleagues. Social workers are obligated to avoid sexual relationships with anyone over whom they have supervisory or administrative authority, including staff they supervise, students, and trainees. As with clients, sexual relationships with colleagues—especially those over whom social workers have authority—can be exploitative and damaging. As in case 3.5, supervisees are typically dependent on their supervisors and could feel pressured to accede to a supervisor's initiation of a sexual relationship to avoid jeopardizing the supervision being provided and the social worker's career advancement.

Students and trainees are especially vulnerable. Social workers who function as classroom and field instructors for social work students exercise considerable control of their students' professional careers and lives in much the same way that supervisors have control over supervisees' lives. Instructors control the grades students receive, and students may feel that their educational and professional careers would be jeopardized if they were to resist instructors' attempts to get involved in a sexual relationship. Thus, social workers should not engage in sexual relationships with any colleague over whom they exercise professional authority, because of the power imbalance and potential for exploitation.

Boundary problems can also emerge when colleagues become involve sexually, as in case 3.6. In this instance, two colleagues became involved at a time when neither had authority over the other. However, during the course of their relationship, which agency administrators did not know about, one of them was promoted to a position that included supervisory authority over the other. In this case the social workers who became involved in an intimate relationship should have taken steps to avoid a conflict of interest, which might have included discussing the situation with the agency director. The parties might have been able to work out an arrangement in which the social worker who was promoted did not have supervisory responsibility over her partner.

NASW *Code of Ethics* standards: Conflicts of Interest (1.06); Consultation (2.05); Sexual Relationships (2.07); Supervision and Consultation (3.01); Education and Training (3.02)

Discussion questions

1. You are a social worker in a juvenile correctional facility. You provide individual and group counseling to juvenile offenders. Over time you become close with one of your social work colleagues with whom you co-facilitate a treatment group. You begin to date and eventually move in together. Would you inform agency supervisors or administrators of your relationship, or would you consider this private information?

2. You are the assistant director of a family service agency. The agency director has asked you to conduct a staff development workshop on the subject of boundaries among agency colleagues. What information and guidelines would you include in your presentation?

Impairment of Colleagues

CASE 3.7. A social work supervisor in a public child welfare agency noticed that one of his social work colleagues occasionally came to work with alcohol on his breath. The two social workers were friendly, although they did not work directly with each other. The supervisor knew that his social work colleague was going through a divorce and having a difficult time emotionally. The supervisor also knew that his colleague had struggled with alcohol abuse in the past.

The supervisor also noticed that his colleague was having difficulty performing some of his job functions; he missed meetings occasionally and often had difficulty meeting routine deadlines. The supervisor was unsure what to say to his colleague, if anything, particularly because he was not his colleague's direct supervisor.

CASE 3.8. A social worker in a group residence for clients with mental retardation had worked with a colleague for nearly 17 years. The social worker noticed that during the past year or so the quality of her colleague's work seemed to deteriorate. He seemed increasingly disinterested in his clients, contributed less and less during staff meetings, called in sick frequently, and seemed to be generally "burned out." Her colleague often complained about his job, administrators, and many colleagues. One day her colleague said at the end of the day, "You know, it's getting harder and harder for me to drag myself into this place. Sometimes I feel like a prisoner crossing the days off his calendar until his release."

Discussion

Social workers occasionally encounter colleagues who are struggling in their own personal lives. As in all professions, social work includes some practitioners whose personal problems affect their ability to perform their professional duties and meet clients' needs. Social workers sometimes become aware that a colleague's emotional, mental health, relationship, family, physical health, financial, legal, substance abuse, or job-related problems are compromising a colleague's judgment and work effectiveness.

Impairment among social workers takes various forms. It may involve failure to provide competent care because of a social worker's alcohol or drug problem (as in case 3.7), severe burnout (as in case 3.8), or because of ethical misconduct (for example, becoming involved in an inappropriate dual relationship with a client). Social workers have an ethical duty to be alert to signs of impairment among colleagues and to consult with those colleagues when feasible about possible remedies and courses of corrective action, particularly when the impairment seems to interfere with the colleague's practice effectiveness. As the NASW *Code of Ethics* states, "Social workers who have direct knowledge of a social work colleague's impairment that is due to personal problems, psychosocial distress, substance abuse, or mental health difficulties and that interferes with practice effectiveness should consult with that colleague when feasible and assist the colleague in taking remedial action" (standard 2.09[a]).

There may be times when a social worker is concerned about a colleague's apparent impairment, but there is no evidence that the impairment affects her or his work. In such instances, social workers must use careful judgment about the appropriateness and likely effectiveness of sharing their concerns with the colleague. When feasible, social workers should use their diplomacy skills to broach this issue, share their concern, and explore constructive ways to address the apparent impairment.

Sometimes social workers who consult with an impaired colleague about their concerns find that the colleague is unwilling to acknowledge or address the problem. In some instances it is not feasible to consult with impaired colleagues because of complex agency dynamics and politics; there may be too much risk to the social worker's own career. In these situations social workers need to consider alternative options to address their concerns about possible harm to clients, such as notifying employers, an agency board of directors, an NASW ethics committee, a licensing or regulatory board, or another professional organization.

NASW *CODE OF ETHICS* STANDARDS: Respect (2.01); Confidentiality (2.02); Consultation (2.05); Impairment of Colleagues (2.09); Impairment (4.05)

DISCUSSION QUESTIONS
1. Two social workers have been colleagues for nearly two years in the mental health unit of a large army base. One of the social workers is concerned that his colleague may be clinically depressed. The colleague's affect has become quite flat, he has lost weight, and his job-related enthusiasm seems to have disappeared. The social worker is concerned about his colleague's ability to help soldiers who struggle with issues in their own lives. What steps might the social worker take to help his colleague?

2. Think about social workers you have known throughout your career as a student or practitioner. How many social work colleagues have you known who seemed to be impaired? What were the signs and symptoms? What steps, if any, did you take to address the apparent impairment? In retrospect, what steps might you have taken?

Incompetence of Colleagues

CASE 3.9. A social worker in a state psychiatric hospital co-facilitated a treatment group with a colleague. The treatment group included patients who were diagnosed with persistent and chronic mental illness and who had difficulty controlling their sexual impulses. All of the patients in the group had behaved inappropriately with people in the community or with other hospital residents.

During the course of their work together, the social worker noticed that his colleague was not familiar with well-known treatment theories and protocols related to this client population. Also, the social worker observed a number of instances when his colleague made insensitive comments to clients about their personal attributes; the colleague also seemed to have difficulty engaging clients clinically. Several of the clients had complained to the social worker privately about his colleague. The social worker had to decide what, if anything, to say to his colleague or supervisors about his concerns.

Discussion

Social workers sometimes encounter colleagues whose professional competence is questionable. This may result from inferior education, poor agency-based and continuing education, or limited skill or aptitude. Social workers who have direct knowledge of a colleague's apparent incompetence should consult with that colleague when feasible and assist the colleague in taking remedial action.

As with impaired colleagues, social workers sometimes find that colleagues are not able or willing to address their incompetence. Social workers who are incompetent in some way, as in case 3.9, may be in denial about their limitations or unwilling to take the time required to enhance their knowledge and skills. When social workers are concerned about the possible impact of a colleague's incompetence on clients, they are ethically obligated to take steps to prevent harm, and this may require bringing their concerns to the attention of employers, an agency board of directors, an NASW ethics committee, a licensing or regulatory board, or another professional organization.

NASW *CODE OF ETHICS* STANDARDS: Respect (2.01); Confidentiality (2.02); Consultation (2.05); Incompetence of Colleagues (2.10); Competence (4.01)

DISCUSSION QUESTIONS

1. You are a social worker in a hospice program that provides supportive services to people who are dying. One of your colleagues is a new employee who has never worked in a hospice program. Over time you discover that while your new colleague has worked in several psychiatric hospitals as a social worker, she has not had much experience working with people who are dying. Your colleague seems unfamiliar with many basic concepts in hospice work related to the emotional challenges faced by people who are dying, changes that occur over time, and common family stressors and dynamics. You offer your colleague some of your resource material, including books and professional journal articles. You also invite your colleague to join you at upcoming continuing education offerings on hospice-related topics. Your colleague seems to be insulted by your gestures and declines your invitations. How would you handle this situation?

2. Think about social workers you have known throughout your career as a student or practitioner. How many social work colleagues have you known who seemed to be incompetent? What were the signs? What steps, if any, did you take to address the apparent incompetence? In retrospect, what steps might you have taken?

Unethical Conduct of Colleagues

CASE 3.10. A social worker at an agency that serves people with physical disabilities administered a program designed to help people remain in their homes and avoid institutional care. The program was funded by a large federal grant.

One year after the program started, the social worker was asked by the agency director to help work on the annual report that the program was required to submit to the federal funding agency. The report included a detailed description of the program's services, personnel, budget, and expenditures.

The social worker reviewed a draft of the report and noticed that the agency's director had seriously misrepresented the way in which the federal funds had been spent. According to the report, the program spent about $62,000 on home-based services that the social worker knew had been spent in other ways, for example, to pay for the agency director's travel to conferences and on office equipment. The social worker was unsure what to do about her discovery.

CASE 3.11. A social worker in private practice began working with a new client who said she wanted some help dealing with a series of what the client described as "failed relationships." The client described several short- and long-term relationships that ended badly. The client said she was eager to explore this pattern and what she might do to prevent a recurrence.

About eight months after they began working together, the client told the social worker that she had something important to share with her. The client tearfully explained that she had not been completely candid with the social worker earlier when the client listed all of her "failed" relationships. The client then disclosed to the social worker that she had omitted one painful relationship, primarily because she was too embarrassed to share the details. The client told the social worker that her most recent relationship had been with the client's former psychotherapist, whom the social worker knows from the local professional community. The client described in detail the nature of her professional, personal, and, eventually, sexual relationship with her former psychotherapist, the social worker's colleague. According to the client, the former therapist and client became sexually involved before the termination of their professional–client relationship.

The client's current social worker told the client that she was "in a real pickle. Certainly I want to help you deal with this; I also have to think about my ethical obligations now that you've told me that one of my colleagues has behaved so unethically." The client pleaded with the social worker to not disclose this information: "I just can't handle that kind of mess. I need to talk to you about this, which is why I brought it up. But I don't want to get him in trouble, and I don't think I could handle the stress."

Discussion

Unfortunately, some social workers—a very small percentage—violate ethical standards in the profession. In this respect, social work is no different from other professions. Examples include social workers who become sexually involved with clients, commit fraud and falsify records, and disclose confidential information improperly.

As in the case of colleagues who appear to be impaired or incompetent, social workers who are concerned about a colleague's unethical behavior are obligated to consider discussing such concerns directly with that colleague. However, direct discussion with a colleague about possible unethical behavior is not always feasible. Social workers may find that colleagues who have engaged in or are engaging in ethical misconduct are in denial about or unwilling to address the problem. Also, practitioners who are aware of a colleague's unethical behavior may feel threatened by the colleague and, consequently, reluctant to discuss their concerns directly with that person. For a variety of reasons, a social worker who is concerned about a colleague's apparent misconduct may feel as if direct discussion with the colleague is not likely to be fruitful.

There are times when social workers are obligated to alert people or organizations in positions of authority to colleagues' unethical behavior. When efforts to resolve unethical behavior through direct discussion with colleagues who appear to have behaved unethically do not succeed, social workers must bring their concerns to the attention of bodies such as state licensing or regulatory boards, an NASW ethics committee, another professional association, or law enforcement agencies.

Decisions about whether to "blow the whistle" on a colleague are very difficult. Social workers generally understand that their obligation to protect clients and the public from unethical social workers may require such action, but they also understand that such disclosure can have serious detrimental repercussions for colleagues whose behavior is reported and, as well, for the social workers who report the unethical behavior. Occasionally whistle-blowers themselves become suspect; their motives may be questioned and their reputations may suffer as a result.

Social workers who consider reporting colleagues' unethical conduct, as in cases 3.10 and 3.11, should take several issues into consideration. Social workers who consider reporting misconduct should examine their own motives to ensure that their goal is to protect clients and the public, as opposed to seeking revenge and retribution against a colleague with whom they have experienced some kind of conflict. Also, social workers should consider how compelling and valid their evidence is. Social workers should think twice about blowing the whistle if their evidence is not reliable, strong, and substantiated.

In addition, social workers should consider whether they have pursued every reasonable alternative in an effort to address their concerns about possible or actual ethical misconduct. These alternatives include direct discussion with the colleague and other pertinent parties. Notification of outside bodies should occur only when other feasible alternatives have been exhausted. Intermediate steps and mediation can be productive, although they do not always succeed.

Finally, social workers should consider how likely it is that bringing a colleague's unethical behavior to the attention of outside authorities will be effective. In some instances outside authorities may be powerless to address the wrongdoing.

NASW *CODE OF ETHICS* STANDARDS: Respect (2.01); Confidentiality (2.02); Consultation (2.05); Unethical Conduct of Colleagues (2.11)

DISCUSSION QUESTIONS

1. You are a social worker in a psychiatric hospital that is in the midst of an accreditation review. The national accreditation organization is planning a five-day site visit to inspect facilities and review programs and services, staffing patterns, health and safety protocols, and clinical records. Two weeks prior to the site visit, your immediate supervisor orders you to rewrite several entries in your and several colleagues' clinical notes. The supervisor explains to you that he reviewed a large sample of the records and concluded that some lack sufficient detail. The supervisor clearly wants you to alter records and embellish clinical details to provide site visitors with a more favorable impression. In your judgment, what the supervisor has asked you to do is to commit fraud. How would you handle this predicament?

2. Think about social workers you have known throughout your career as a student or practitioner. How many social work colleagues have you known who seemed to be unethical? What were the signs? What steps, if any, did you take to address the apparent unethical behavior? In retrospect, what steps might you have taken?

chapter four

Ethical Responsibilities in Practice Settings

Social workers sometimes encounter challenging ethical dilemmas in the workplace. Common dilemmas concern supervision; consultation; education and training; performance evaluation; client records; billing; client transfer; administration; continuing education; staff development; commitments to employers; and labor–management disputes.

Supervision and Consultation

CASE 4.1. A social worker in an employee assistance program supervised a recent MSW graduate who was also new in town. Over time the two became friendly. The supervisor and her husband occasionally invited the supervisee to their home for dinner. Eventually the supervisor introduced the supervisee to the supervisor's son and the two began dating. The supervisee spent increasing amounts of time with her supervisor and her family.

CASE 4.2. A social worker was hired by the executive director of a mental health center to formulate and deliver a comprehensive staff development program for agency staffers. The consultant is an MSW with extensive experience in the continuing education field. The agency director hired the social worker after reviewing three proposals submitted by area professionals who specialize in staff development.

Earlier in their careers the executive director and the social worker whose proposal was approved were colleagues at a nearby psychiatric hospital. They have been close friends ever since. The executive director did not disclose this fact to any of his administrative colleagues at the agency or to the agency's board of directors.

Discussion

Supervision and consultation have always been essential social work functions. Supervision can occur for clinical, case management, or administrative staff. Consultation can occur within an agency or through outside consultants.

As in relationships with clients and colleagues, social work supervisors and consultants must maintain proper boundaries in their relationships with supervisees and consultants. In principle, supervisees can be exploited or harmed by dual and multiple relationships. As discussed earlier, supervisors exercise some form of authority over supervisees, and this imbalance of power can lead to exploitation or harm if supervisors do not handle it properly. Furthermore, relationships with consultants must be managed carefully to avoid conflicts of interest and impropriety.

Dual and multiple relationships between supervisors and supervisees, and between consultants and their clients, can take various forms, including personal, religious, political, or business relationships. Supervisors and consultants should avoid dual relationships that have the potential to interfere with the quality and objectivity of their supervision and consultation. In case 4.1, for example, the social work supervisor may have found it increasingly difficult to be objective in her supervision, due to the blossoming relationship that was developing between her son and her supervisee. More specifically, this kind of dual relationship can compromise the quality of the supervisor's performance evaluation. Because of the considerable consequences often associated with job-based evaluations, supervisors must evaluate supervisees' performance in a manner that is, and is perceived to be, fair. This protects both supervisees, clients, and the broader public. Evaluations that exaggerate a supervisee's skills, perhaps due to favoritism that arises out of a dual relationship, could lead to unwarranted promotions and, ultimately, could place that social worker in increasingly responsible positions for which she or he is not qualified, thus exposing clients and others to risk.

In case 4.2, it was unethical for the agency director to award his good friend a contract to develop and implement a staff development program without disclosing his personal relationship to the consultant and without involving other agency administrators or the board of directors.

In addition to being concerned about acts of impropriety, social work supervisors and consultants also need to be concerned about the appearance of impropriety. Although actual impropriety is patently problematic, the mere appearance of impropriety can have dire consequences. Understandably, other staffers involved in case 4.1 may have been upset by the close personal relationship developing between the social work supervisor and her supervisee. Other staffers may have been concerned about favoritism, which can have an adverse impact on agency staffers' morale. Similarly, the possibility of favoritism in case 4.2 can lead to suspicions that the agency director sacrificed quality to award a lucrative contract to his close friend. Not only can this kind of favoritism harm agency morale, it can lead to awarding contracts to less qualified and skilled consultants.

NASW *Code of Ethics* standards: Conflicts of Interest (1.06); Consultation (2.05); Sexual Relationships (2.07); Supervision and Consultation (3.01); Education and Training (3.02); Performance Evaluation (3.03)

Discussion questions
1. You are the administrator of a community mental health center. What guidelines and procedures would you establish to ensure proper boundaries between agency-based supervisors and their supervisees?
2. You are the administrator of a hospital-based hospice program. What guidelines and procedures would you establish to ensure proper boundaries between the agency and outside consultants?

Education and Training

Case 4.3. A social work field instructor at a family services agency supervised a social work student enrolled in a local graduate school. The student was assigned to work with foster parents who sought advice about how best to manage foster children's challenging behavior.

The field instructor met with the student to review some of the most challenging behaviors that come to the agency's attention and to learn about various behavior management techniques and protocols that foster parents often find helpful. Toward the end of their meeting, the field instructor told the student that he is not to tell foster parents that he is a student. According to the field instructor, "In the past we've found that foster parents sometimes object when a student is assigned to work with them. We've also found that foster parents tend to respect the students more when they think they're regular employees."

Case 4.4. A social work field instructor at a nursing home supervised a BSW student. The two had a very good working relationship. About halfway through the field placement the field instructor learned that she would need kidney-replacement surgery. The field instructor shared the news with the student, and the two of them discussed supervision options. Toward the end of the conversation, the field instructor told the student that her doctors were having considerable difficulty finding a donor with an acceptable antigen match. The student decided to have herself tested as a possible donor. To everyone's surprise, the student was identified as a suitable donor. The field instructor was delighted to hear the news but uncertain about accepting a kidney from her student.

CASE 4.5. A professor in an undergraduate social work education program taught a course on community organizing. One of his students was especially talented and had a strong interest in community organizing.

The professor worked part-time for a large community development program that had a large grant to organize the local community to address the lack of affordable housing. The professor administered this project and provided staff with supervision. The project had an opening for a part-time community organizer. The professor's student saw an ad for the position and applied for it. The professor was unsure about whether he could hire his student.

Discussion

Several ethical standards pertain to social work education and training. One of these standards concerns clients' right to know about their social worker's professional experience, educational background, and credentials. As in case 4.3, such information is important to some clients and is a key component in their consent to services. In this regard, clients have the right to know when they are being served by students who, by definition, have not yet completed their formal social work education. Although many clients do not object to being served by students, some may prefer more experienced practitioners. Although professionals in training must have access to clients and patients to develop their knowledge and skills, clients and patients nonetheless have a right to express preferences and make informed choices with respect to the background and credentials of the professionals who care for them.

Thus, social workers who function as educators and field instructors for students should take reasonable steps to ensure that clients are routinely informed when services are being provided by students. Social work educators, field instructors, and the students themselves must be careful not to mislead clients or misrepresent the nature of students' background and credentials. Agencies in which students conduct their field work should establish policies to ensure that clients are informed, either in writing or orally, that they are being served by students (see NASW *Code of Ethics* standard 3.02[c]).

Social work educators and field instructors must also pay close to attention to dual relationships with students, as in cases 4.4 and 4.5. Dual and multiple relationships between social work educators and students can occur in various ways. For example, social work educators may have friends, relatives, neighbors, or former colleagues enroll in their program. In some circumstances, as in case 4.5, a social work student may be in a position to provide a valuable favor for the field instructor.

Some dual and multiple relationships between social work educators and students are unethical and some are not. As with any dual or multiple relationship, the challenge is to avoid any relationship that involves a risk of exploitation or potential harm to the person in the subordinate position in the relationship. In case 4.4, the student certainly has the right to donate her kidney to the field instructor if she so wishes. In fact, such generosity is admirable. The field instructor, in turn, would have a duty to ensure that this dual relationship unfolds consistent with prevailing ethical standards. One possibility would be for the field instructor to terminate her formal supervision relationship with the student and arrange, with the student's consent, for a colleague to assume the field instruction duties.

In case 4.5, the social work professor would need to be careful to avoid any conflict of interest. It could be problematic for the professor to serve simultaneously as the student's classroom instructor and employment supervisor. Although it is possible that no conflict would arise, there is a possibility that it would. To avoid a conflict of interest—for example, the student might be concerned that the quality of his or her work as an employee somehow might affect his or her school grade assigned by the professor—the professor might make an arrangement to avoid any direct supervision of the student in his role as employee.

NASW *Code of Ethics* standards: Conflicts of Interest (1.06); Consultation (2.05); Sexual Relationships (2.07); Supervision and Consultation (3.01); Education and Training (3.02); Performance Evaluation (3.03)

Discussion questions

1. You are a social worker in a hospital. Your responsibilities include supervising a field unit for the local school of social work. Ordinarily you supervise between three and five students. What policies and procedures would you establish regarding information that social work students provide to hospital patients about their student status?

2. Social work field instructors and students sometimes give each other gifts. Assume you are a field instructor. What would your policy be with regard to giving gifts to, and receiving gifts from, students?

3. Suppose you are a social work professor who has a contract to conduct a program evaluation for a local community action program. One of your students is very interested in research and is quite skilled. Would you be willing to hire your student? How would you prevent complicated boundary issues?

Client Records

CASE 4.6. A social worker at a community mental health center provided services to struggling adolescents. One of the social worker's clients was referred by a local school. According to school personnel, the student was sullen, withdrawn, and having significant academic problems. The school's vice principal told the social worker that the student was very upset because his father was recently sentenced to prison for drug dealing and his mother was having psychiatric problems.

On the basis of the strict criteria in the *Diagnostic and Statistical Manual of Mental Disorders*, the student's clinical symptoms were not serious enough to qualify for insurance coverage. To qualify for insurance coverage, the social worker would need to exaggerate the students' clinical symptoms.

CASE 4.7. A social worker at a family services agency was sued by a former client. The former client, who attempted to commit suicide and was hospitalized following the unsuccessful attempt, alleged that the social worker failed to intervene properly when the woman manifested symptoms of suicidal ideation.

After receiving the lawsuit, the social worker reviewed her clinical record. To the social worker's dismay, she discovered that she had not documented a telephone call she had made to a psychiatrist just prior to the woman's crisis to consult about management of the client's suicidal ideation. The social worker was tempted to insert a brief note about the telephone call at the end of the clinical note she had written just prior to the former client's suicide attempt.

CASE 4.8. A social worker in a residential substance abuse treatment program provided counseling services to a 32-year-old man who struggled with heroin addiction. During one counseling session the client told the social worker that as part of his recovery he felt the need to be honest about mistakes he has made in the past. He told the social worker about the extent of his past drug use and drug dealing. At one point in the conversation the client took a deep breath, began to cry, and told the social worker that nine years earlier he had murdered another drug dealer who had tried to rob the client. The client told the social worker that no one knows that he was the murderer. The client said to the social worker, "I assume this secret is safe with you. I just had to tell someone, and you're someone I know I can trust."

Discussion

Documentation is one of the most important skills in social work. Careful and skilled documentation is essential to identify, describe, and assess clients' needs; define the purposes of services and interventions; document services provided, goals, plans, activities, and progress; provide proper supervision; and evaluate the effectiveness of services and interventions.

It is important for social workers to include timely and accurate documentation in case records. Social workers should not falsify records or record inaccurate information. In case 4.6, for example, it would be unethical for the social worker to embellish or exaggerate a client's clinical symptoms. It is certainly understandable that a social worker might want to bend the rules to help the client qualify for insurance reimbursement. However, such fraud is problematic in two respects. First, the social worker may inadvertently convey to the client that fraud is acceptable; this is poor role modeling and can undermine clients' efforts to address integrity and other moral issues in their own lives. Second, such deception exposes social workers to potential fraud allegations, litigation, and ethics complaints.

It would also be unethical for the social worker in case 4.7 to alter her clinical note after the fact to indicate that she had telephoned the psychiatrist to consult about managing the former client's suicidal ideation. Assuming the social worker did, in fact, call the psychiatrist and is not creating a false entry to protect herself in the litigation, the ethical course of action would be for the social worker to add a new clinical note with the **current** date indicating that in reviewing the clinical record and past entries the social worker discovered that she neglected to document the telephone call she made to the psychiatrist at an earlier date. The social worker could then document the telephone call the same way she would have had she entered the note contemporaneously. This way of handling the ethical dilemma is forthright, in that it acknowledges the late entry and documents the telephone call accurately.

Accurate documentation does not necessarily mean that social workers are obligated to record every detail shared with them by clients. To protect clients to the

101

greatest extent possible under the law and prevailing ethical standards, social workers should record information with the understanding that other parties—such as lawyers, utilization review and insurance staffers, agency colleagues, law enforcement officials, judges, and jurors—may eventually have access to that information. Also, social workers should not include any gratuitous or tangential information in the case record. Only information that is directly relevant to the clients' issues or problems and the services provided should be included. Practitioners should omit excessively subjective or speculative observations for which there is little or no empirical evidence or documentation. The record also should not contain gossip; derogatory language; or information about a client's political, religious, or other personal views, unless such details are directly relevant to treatment.

With regard to case 4.8, generally speaking social workers should not include details of past crimes committed by clients or of crimes they are currently committing. Including such information may violate clients' right to confidentiality and, as well, violate federal and other laws that require strict protection of health- and substance abuse-related information. Such information might be included, however, if doing so is required by law or the information is critical to the delivery of services (for example, when social workers who are probation or parole officers are required to report clients' illegal activities, when clients disclose that they have abused a child or elderly person, or when a client has threatened to murder someone).

As discussed earlier, ethical and legal guidelines generally permit or require social workers to disclose confidential information without clients' consent when such disclosure is necessary to prevent serious, imminent, and foreseeable harm to a third party. In case 4.8, it is likely that the social worker's documentation or disclosure of facts related to the murder would not meet this standard, in that documentation or disclosure is not likely to prevent serious, imminent, and foreseeable harm, assuming the social worker has no evidence to suggest that the client poses a threat currently.

NASW *CODE OF ETHICS* STANDARDS: Commitment to Clients (1.01); Informed Consent (1.03); Privacy and Confidentiality (1.07); Consultation (2.05); Client Records (3.04); Billing (3.05); Dishonesty, Fraud, and Deception (4.04)

DISCUSSION QUESTIONS

1. You are a social worker in private practice. One of your clients is in the middle of a contentious divorce and child custody dispute. During one confidential counseling session the client disclosed to you that during his

marriage he became involved in a sexual relationship with another man. The client talked about his growing sense that he is bisexual. What information would you include in your clinical case notes?

2. One of your private practice clients sought counseling to help him deal with distress he experienced after his long-time partner ended their relationship. The man was eager to explore the problematic dynamics in the relationship. The client had little money to pay for counseling services; unfortunately, his employer's insurance company does not cover counseling for the man's symptoms. The man asked you if there might be some way to "write up my problem to make the insurance company happy so they'll be willing to pay your bill." How would you respond?

Client Transfer

CASE 4.9. A social worker in private practice was contacted by a man who said he was trying to find a therapist to help him deal with the end of a long-term relationship. The man explained to the social worker that he had been in counseling with another therapist for about six months and felt like he "no longer clicked" with that therapist. The social worker agreed to meet with the man and asked him whether he had terminated with his other therapist and what he had told the other therapist about the reasons for termination. The man said that he had not yet said anything to his other therapist but would do so once he located a new therapist with whom he is comfortable.

Discussion

People who are receiving clinical services from other professionals in the community will sometimes contact a social worker in their efforts to find a different clinician. This may occur because the individuals are not entirely satisfied with their current clinician.

To meet clients' needs and avoid conflicts of interest and conflicts with colleagues, social workers should discuss with potential clients the nature of their current relationship with other clinicians and the possible benefits and risks of transferring to a new clinician. It is important for social workers to avoid undermining or interfering with clients' relationships with other professionals and to avoid engaging in any activity that could be interpreted as an effort to lure clients away from colleagues. Social workers should not exploit potential clients' disputes with their current clinicians to advance their own interests. A social worker should accept a new client who is working with other providers only when it is clear that the client is aware of the possible ramifications—both positive and negative—of entering into a new professional–client relationship and when such a relationship appears to be in the client's best interest. On one hand, potential clients may find it useful to embark on a new therapeutic relationship with a clinician whose work is based on a different conceptual framework and theories and who uses different clinical interventions and techniques. Clients who feel as if they are not making significant progress may find this change of approach and perspective quite productive. On the other hand, transitioning to a new clinician also has its risks. Clients may lose clinical momentum and may have to revisit issues in ways that are unproductive. Also, terminating with a therapist can be traumatic regardless of the reasons for termination.

NASW *Code of Ethics* standards: Commitment to Clients (1.01); Self-Determination (1.02); Conflicts of Interest (1.06); Respect (2.01); Consultation (2.05); Referral for Services (2.06); Client Transfer (3.06)

Discussion questions
1. Suppose you are the social worker in case 4.9 who receives a telephone call from a man who has been working with another clinician and is interested in transferring to you. Describe the conversation you think you would have with this man about the possibility of changing therapists.
2. Assume that you agree to work with the man in case 4.9. The client explains that he has had a "falling out" with his former therapist and does not want you to contact her to discuss the client's clinical issues and will not sign a release authorizing the former therapist to share with you a copy of the client's clinical record. How would you respond? Would you be willing to work with this client under these circumstances?

Administration

Case 4.10. A social worker who was the director of a program for people who are homeless was notified by one of her key funding agencies, the county department of human services, of a 45 percent cut in grant monies due to a fiscal crisis. The decrease in funding devastated the agency's budget and required significant cutbacks in the agency's program and services. The director assembled her senior staff to think through which shelter, counseling, and health care services would be eliminated and how the remaining funds would be allocated.

CASE 4.11. A newly appointed executive director of a crisis program for teenagers met with each of the agency's assistant directors and program directors in an effort to learn more about the agency's services, strengths, and challenges. During their meeting, the director of the agency's substance abuse counseling program informed the executive director, a social worker, that the former executive director had embellished many of the service-utilization statistics reported in the most recent quarterly report submitted to the state mental health agency that provides most of the agency's funds. According to the director of the agency's substance abuse counseling program, the former executive director was worried about the significant decline in the number of clients served by the agency and was concerned that this might lead the state agency to cut its funding. The current executive director investigated the allegation and verified that it was true. She had to decide how to handle this discovery.

Discussion

Social work administrators frequently encounter ethical dilemmas involving the allocation of limited agency resources, dual relationships, conflicts of interest, and ethical misconduct. Their management of these challenging circumstances can have a profound impact on an agency's functioning and ability to meet clients' needs.

As in case 4.10, social work administrators are responsible for distributing resources that are often scarce. Some scarce resources are allocated to clients (such as counseling appointments, emergency shelter beds and subsidized housing units, and food vouchers), and others are distributed to staff (such as salaries, promotions, travel expenses, educational leave opportunities, and office equipment).

Social work administrators who are responsible for distributing limited or scarce resources should attempt to implement resource allocation criteria and procedures that are open and fair. Whatever distribution mechanism administrators choose should be discussed openly among staff and, when appropriate, clients. Resources should not be allocated in an arbitrary, capricious, or discriminatory manner. Rather, there should be a sound, fair, and conceptually based rationale for the criteria and mechanisms used to allocate resources to promote what moral philosophers call "distributive justice."

The administrator in case 4.10 has taken an important first step by assembling her senior staff to consider how to allocate the agency's reduced and limited funds. In principle, the administrator and her staff have several options. They could allocate the agency's available funds equally or rank order the agency's programs on the basis of their sense of the most compelling needs addressed by the various programs. Sometimes social workers allocate limited resources, in part, on the basis of affirmative-action principles to ensure that vulnerable ethnic subgroups and people of color receive important services.

Historically, social workers and others have had difficulty reaching consensus about the fairest way to allocate resources. Some prefer allocation procedures that emphasize equality; others favor criteria that give priority to those most in need or those who are victims of racism, discrimination, or other forms of oppression. Generally, however, social workers agree that they should strive to establish allocation procedures that are open, fair, nondiscriminatory, and based on consistently applied conceptual criteria. When appropriate, clients, staff, and members of the public (neighborhoods, communities) should be invited to participate in the development of allocation criteria.

It is critically important for social work administrators to be familiar with widely held ethical standards in the profession and to incorporate them into their administrative tasks. Administrators should assess the extent to which their agencies and organizations comply with these ethical standards and develop policies and procedures that reflect them. They should take reasonable steps to ensure that their agencies and organizations adhere to these ethical standards.

In addition to developing and implementing policies and procedures that enhance agencies' and organizations' compliance with ethical standards, social work administrators also should attempt to eliminate any conditions in their work settings that violate, interfere with, or discourage compliance with these standards. This is the task facing the administrator in case 4.11, who discovered that her predecessor had falsified service-utilization statistics.

For both moral and self-interested reasons, it would be difficult for the administrator in case 4.11 to ignore her discovery of the falsified statistics. Morally, it would be unethical to conceal falsified statistics that were transmitted to the state agency that provided public funds to the program. Although there may be repercussions for the agency, ethically the administrator should take the honorable step of notifying state officials of her discovery and then attempt to negotiate a resolution that minimizes negative repercussions for the agency. Furthermore, the administrator might expose herself to risk if she does not disclose the falsified data. If state officials discover the deception on their own, the current administrator could be accused of knowingly covering up the deception. This could have legal consequences and harm her professional career.

NASW *CODE OF ETHICS* STANDARDS: Commitment to Clients (1.01); Conflicts of Interest (1.06); Consultation (2.05); Unethical Conduct of Colleagues (2.11); Administration (3.07); Commitment to Employers (3.09); Dishonesty, Fraud, and Deception (4.04)

DISCUSSION QUESTIONS

1. You are the director of a program that makes subsidized apartments available for low-income people. Your agency receives federal and state funds to subsidize rents, which enables your agency to provide housing to people for below-market rents. Your city has a high unemployment rate, severe economic problems, and many people without shelter. In the current funding cycle, your agency will be able to subsidize apartments to 35 families. However, 97 families have applied for the 35 apartments. What criteria and procedures would you use to allocate the limited number of apartments?

2. You are hired as the director of a food bank that serves a large metropolitan area with a population of about 500,000 people. Your agency's budget includes federal and state funds, in addition to private donations. Two months after you are hired, you discover that the food bank's chief financial officer has embezzled approximately $27,000 of the agency's funds. How would you handle this situation?

Commitments to Employers

CASE 4.12. A social worker was hired by a group home that provides crisis services to adolescent girls. The group home operated under the auspices of a large church. At the time she was hired, the social worker signed an agreement stating that she would not discuss abortion with pregnant clients or refer them for abortion services. About 10 months after she was hired, a 16-year-old group home resident informed the social worker that she is pregnant. The girl told the social worker that she wanted some help thinking through all of her options, including parenting the baby herself, placing the baby in an adoptive home, and abortion. The social worker was personally "pro-choice" but was uneasy about discussing abortion in light of the agreement she had signed.

CASE 4.13. A social worker was employed by a federally funded agency that provides child care, preschool education, and social services to low-income children and families. To receive the agency's services, families must meet certain income eligibility criteria. According to agency policy and federal guidelines, the agency is not allowed to serve any family whose income exceeded certain thresholds.

The social worker met with and reviewed an application submitted by a refugee family with two young children. The family had emigrated to the United States because of political persecution in their homeland. The parents worked several jobs to make ends meet; as a result, their income exceeded the program's limits. The social worker felt that the family was being treated unjustly. She admired the parents' earnest attempt to support the family and was eager to do everything possible to help them. The social worker considered underreporting the family's income so they would qualify for the agency's services, although she knew this would violate both agency and federal policies.

Discussion

Generally speaking, social workers should support their employers' policies and honor their agreements with them. Organizational loyalty is important to enhance trust among employees and administrators, minimize conflict, and enhance overall agency functioning. Deliberate violation of agency policies can be terribly disruptive organizationally and, in addition, harm the social worker's and the profession's reputations.

That said, social workers sometimes encounter unique and extreme circumstances when they may need to consider breaking commitments they have made to employers and employing organizations on moral grounds, based on social work's core values, ethical principles, and ethical standards. Occasionally, organizations engage in unethical practices and implement unethical policies. When this occurs, social workers have a moral duty to challenge these practices and policies and may need to consider breaking commitments they have made to employers. As I asserted in the discussion of whistle-blowing, social workers should be both cautious and circumspect in these situations and should carefully examine their motives, the quality of their evidence of wrongdoing, the magnitude of the issue and possible consequences, and whether insubordination is a last resort.

Social workers who break commitments to their employers must be willing to accept the possible consequences. In case 4.12, for example, if the social worker believes that she has a duty to give information to the adolescent about all of her legal options—without pressuring the youth to pursue any one of them—the social worker should first share her concerns with administrators. If administrators are not persuaded, the social worker could consider resigning her position because of her unwillingness to comply with what she regards as an unethical policy. One might argue that the social worker would have been wise to not pursue a job in an agency that followed a policy that the social worker considered unacceptable and indefensible.

In case 4.13, in contrast, the social worker might not have been able to anticipate the moral problem she encountered regarding enforcement of the income eligibility criteria for people applying for services. In both cases the social workers face difficult decisions of conscience.

Deciding whether to honor or violate one's commitment to employers in the face of seemingly unethical practices and policies is one of the most daunting ethical challenges social workers encounter. These ethical dilemmas are comparable to those involving civil disobedience, that is, when citizens decide whether deliberate violation of laws and regulations is justifiable on moral grounds. It is difficult to provide unambiguous and explicit guidance about when it is and is not ethical for social workers to violate agency policy.

Ideally, social workers should try to prevent these difficult ethical choices by seeking to improve or modify their employers' allegedly unjust policies and procedures. One way to do this is to identify, review, and monitor agencies' policies and procedures to ensure that they are ethical. This can be especially challenging in interdisciplinary settings where social work is not the primary profession, such as in schools, hospitals, correctional institutions, and the military. In these settings administrators and colleagues from other professions may not be familiar with, or entirely supportive of, social work values and ethical standards. When this occurs, social workers should do their best to acquaint colleagues with social work values and standards and social workers' obligation to adhere to them. Social workers can begin this process informally by discussing their concerns with appropriate colleagues and administrators. Informal efforts to resolve problematic policies, procedures, regulations, and administrative orders are often successful. However, when such informal efforts do not succeed, social workers should consider taking more formal steps within their agencies and organizations, perhaps by bringing their concerns to the attention of supervisors and administrators and request a formal response. When feasible and necessary, social workers may also contact an agency's board of directors. If these efforts are not fruitful, social workers should consider whether the ethics-related problems are sufficiently serious to warrant bringing the matter to the attention of parties outside the organization, such as an advocacy group, a regulatory body, or the media.

NASW *CODE OF ETHICS* STANDARDS: Commitment to Clients (1.01); Consultation (2.05); Administration (3.07); Commitments to Employers (3.09); Dishonesty, Fraud, and Deception (4.04)

DISCUSSION QUESTIONS

1. You are a social worker at a state public welfare department. The state's governor issued a directive requiring that all state employees disclose the names of any clients or applicants for services who appear to be undocumented immigrants. The governor has announced that his office will take steps to deport these individuals. You are concerned about violating clients' right to confidentiality and privacy. You are also concerned that complying with the governor's directive will harm the agency's reputation and diminish clients' trust. How would you handle this situation?

2. You are the social worker in case 4.12. Personally, you believe in pregnant women's right to choose whether to carry a pregnancy to term, place the baby with adoptive parents, or terminate the pregnancy. How would you handle the situation in this case?

Labor–Management Disputes

CASE 4.14. A social worker at a large urban hospital was notified by the social work department's director that the union representing hospital nurses was about to go on strike. For several months the union and hospital representatives had been negotiating a new contract, but negotiations recently fell apart. The strike was scheduled to begin the following day.

The hospital's social workers met to discuss the situation. Some of the social workers felt strongly that they should support the nurses, whose wages and benefits lagged behind those in other area hospitals; other social workers argued vehemently that the social workers should not abandon the hospital's patients and had a duty to cross the picket line and report for work.

Discussion

There is a long and close connection between the social work profession and organized labor. Throughout social work's history, practitioners have been involved extensively in the formation and operation of unions. Some social workers have been employed in unions that work on behalf of organized groups, such as laborers, factory workers, and municipal employees.

There has been vigorous debate among social workers about the relationship between social work ethics and the labor movement's mission and strategies. Some social workers believe that unions' traditional commitment to protecting and serving vulnerable and sometimes oppressed workers is a compelling extension of the profession's values. Other social workers maintain that unions sometimes place members' self-serving interests (for example, concerning wages, benefits, and working conditions) above clients' interests.

The majority of social workers acknowledge that unions perform a very important function in the profession by helping maintain worker morale and, ultimately, promoting and enhancing working conditions. Unions' advocacy on behalf of social workers and their efforts to improve professionals' morale and working conditions can enhance practitioners' ability to serve clients and meet their needs.

The current NASW *Code of Ethics* is the first of the profession's codes to directly address labor–management disputes.

> Social workers may engage in organized action, including the formation of and participation in labor unions, to improve services to clients and working conditions. (standard 3.10[a])

> The actions of social workers who are involved in labor–management disputes, job actions, or labor strikes should be guided by the profession's values, ethical principles, and ethical standards. Reasonable differences of opinion exist among social workers concerning their primary obligation as professionals during an actual or threatened labor strike or job action. Social workers should carefully examine relevant issues and their possible impact on clients before deciding on a course of action. (standard 3.10[b])

Clearly, the code recognizes the complexity of social workers' decisions to participate in an actual or threatened labor strike or job action. On one hand, social workers are obligated to uphold their commitment to clients, whose needs might go unmet or neglected during a labor strike or job action. On the other hand, exercising the right to strike and engage in job actions may be necessary to sustain social workers' morale and promote working conditions that enhance practitioners' ability to meet clients' needs. As the code states, reasonable differences of opinion exist among social workers concerning their primary obligation in these circumstances.

NASW *Code of Ethics* STANDARDS: Commitment to Clients (1.01); Conflicts of Interest (1.06); Consultation (2.05); Administration (3.07); Commitments to Employers (3.09); Labor–Management Disputes (3.10); Public Emergencies (6.03)

DISCUSSION QUESTIONS

1. You are the director of social work at the hospital in case 4.14. You have just been informed that the hospital's nurses have declared a strike and set up a picket line. What advice would you give the social workers on your staff about reporting to work or respecting the picket line?

2. The NASW *Code of Ethics* states that "reasonable differences of opinion exist among social workers concerning their primary obligation as professionals during an actual or threatened labor strike or job action." The code does not take an explicit position for or against social workers' support of a strike but, rather, encourages social workers to examine all "relevant issues and their possible impact on clients" before making a decision. Do you agree with this ethical standard? Do you think the code should take a firmer position on this issue?

chapter five

Ethical Responsibilities as Professionals

Social workers sometimes encounter ethical dilemmas concerning their responsibilities as professionals. Among the most common are those involving social workers' professional competence; private conduct; honesty; impairment; solicitation of clients from other professionals; and acknowledgment of work done by professional colleagues.

Professional Competence

CASE 5.1. A social worker in private practice provided services to children, adolescents, and families. The social worker had considerable expertise related to child behavior management and parent–child conflict.

One afternoon the social worker received a call from an adoptive mother who explained that she and her husband needed help navigating a complex "open" adoption. The social worker was not very familiar with the concept of open adoption; nonetheless, the social worker arranged to meet with the parents.

During their first meeting the parents explained to the social worker that they adopted their three-year-old child at birth. They had two face-to-face meetings with the birth mother before the birth and have had occasional telephone contact since. The parents explained that they sought an open adoption because of their belief that it is in their child's best interest.

The parents told the social worker that they continue to believe in open adoption and would like some help thinking through what kind of relationship to maintain with their child's birth mother—what kind of contact (for example, in-person visits, telephone contact, e-mail contact), the frequency and location of contacts, and so on. The social worker knew that several social workers in the area specialized in work with adoptive families and that two of them had considerable expertise related to open adoption, had received extensive continuing education on the subject, and were familiar with pertinent literature. The social worker felt confident that she could help the parents but wondered whether she should refer them to one of her colleagues who specialized in open adoption.

Discussion

In general, social workers should offer professional services only when they have proper education, training, knowledge, and skills. To do otherwise would be irresponsible. Social workers should have at least minimally acceptable competence to meet clients' needs and perform the duties required by their employers.

In some instances social workers clearly should not hold themselves out as experts, for example, when a social worker whose education and experience have focused exclusively on the delivery of services to the elderly considers applying for a job as a social worker in a substance abuse treatment program. Clients in the substance abuse treatment program would not be well served by a social worker who has no formal education, training, or experience in the field.

However, other circumstances, as in case 5.1, are less clear. On occasion, social workers may have reasonable expertise to provide services to clients but may not be the most qualified practitioners available. In these situations, and assuming social workers work in a community where more qualified practitioners are available, social workers should explain to clients the nature and extent of their expertise, provide an overview of practitioners in the area who may have more expertise, explain their own strengths and limitations with regard to meeting the clients' needs, encourage the clients to ask questions, and then encourage clients to make an informed decision about which practitioner would be most appropriate. This approach is consistent with the concept of informed consent.

Like all professionals, social workers should constantly seek ways to strengthen and upgrade their knowledge and skills throughout their careers. Even the best undergraduate and graduate social work education programs can provide students with only foundation-level knowledge and skills and a moderate amount of advanced content. The amount of time social workers spend in formal education is a modest fraction of the time spent learning throughout their careers. During the course of their careers, social workers can expect to encounter new conceptual models and intervention approaches; practitioners must always be open to learning.

If the social worker in case 5.1 ends up assuming responsibility for the clients who sought her help, she would have a duty to learn as much as possible about clinical issues related to open adoption. This would require considerable effort. One attribute of professionalism is the willingness to draw on relevant bodies of knowledge. Social workers have a responsibility to consult the literature pertinent to their practice areas. This includes nonempirical and empirical literature. Nonempirical literature includes theoretical and conceptual discussions, in this case concerning the nature of, the dynamics involved in, and ways of defining and negotiating an open adoption. Nonempirical literature does not include analyses of data based on formal observation. Empirical knowledge, in contrast, draws on and presents data or statistics pertaining to the subject matter. The data may be qualitative or quantitative and are obtained by such techniques as interviews, questionnaires, structured observations, formal assessments, and paper-and-pencil tests.

NASW *Code of Ethics* standards: Commitment to Clients (1.01); Informed Consent (1.03); Competence (1.04 and 4.01); Conflicts of Interest (1.06); Consultation (2.05); Referral for Services (2.06); Incompetence of Colleagues (2.10); Misrepresentation (4.06)

Discussion questions

1. You are a clinical social worker who specializes in the treatment of anxiety disorders. One of your clients, who has been diagnosed with posttraumatic stress disorder, has also developed an eating disorder. You do not have a great deal of experience treating eating disorders, but would like to learn more about them. What specific resources would you try to locate to enhance your knowledge? Where would you go to find these resources?

2. What specific steps do you take, or plan to take, to update your knowledge and skills throughout your career? What are the different ways for social workers to obtain continuing education?

Private Conduct

Case 5.2. A social worker in private practice counseled a couple who were having marital difficulties. According to the couple, most of their conflict arose out of the challenges they faced parenting their adolescent son who struggled with depression, behavioral challenges, and academic difficulties. During the course of their work together, the social worker referred the couple to an educational consultant who might be able to help the family locate a specialized school for their son. The educational consultant eventually recommended placement of the child in an alternative high school located in a neighboring community. As part of the school's program, the students' parents participated in monthly meetings that functioned as a support group and provided an opportunity for parents to talk about their personal challenges that might affect their children (such as marital, mental health, and addiction issues).

Coincidentally, the social worker's son also attended this school. The social worker and his wife attended the monthly meetings, during which they had disclosed some personal information about their family's life. The social worker was uneasy about attending these meetings with his clients present.

CASE 5.3. A social worker at a family services agency provided counseling to a 45-year-old woman who sought help following the termination of a long-term intimate relationship. In therapy the client spent considerable time talking about the difficulty she has had over the years maintaining healthy, stable intimate relationships.

The social worker was an active member of her local church, a large congregation with nearly 3,200 parishioners, one of whom was the client. Ordinarily the social worker and client did not encounter each other at church.

At the end of a recent worship service, the minister announced a new capital campaign for the church and invited parishioners to contact the church office if they wished to join the campaign committee, which would be chaired by the social worker. The minister announced that the newly appointed committee would hold its first meeting at the chair's home in two weeks.

Unbeknown to the social worker, the client had telephoned the church office to sign up for the committee. The client appeared at the social worker's home for the first meeting. The social worker was concerned about mixing her personal and professional lives, the client's presence in her home, and the potential impact on her relationship with her client.

CASE 5.4. A social worker recently moved to a rural community after she was hired as the director of casework services at a prominent social services agency. Throughout her career in two other large cities the social worker had been very involved in politics. In one city the social worker served on the city council and in the other city the social worker chaired a political action committee.

The social worker, who happened to be lesbian, was invited by a statewide political committee to be a candidate for the state legislature, a part-time position. The social worker expected that her well-known sexual orientation and history of political activism would arise during the course of a campaign. She wondered what impact this might have on her employer and clients.

Discussion

Ordinarily, what social workers do in their private lives is a personal matter and does not intersect with their professional lives. Certainly social workers should have the freedom to pursue their social, religious, and recreational interests. However, social workers sometimes encounter challenging issues when their private and professional lives intersect.

In some instances, social workers must be careful to separate their personal and professional lives. For example, in case 5.2 it would not be appropriate for the social worker to participate in a support group with his clients that is sponsored by the specialized school that their respective children attend. Ordinarily parents in this support group share personal information about their personal and family lives. In this unique situation the social worker would need to discuss the boundary issues with the parents to ensure that they understand why the social worker needs to separate his personal life and professional work. Ideally, with the clients' consent the social worker would need to explain the unusual situation to the school's staffers and discuss appropriate alternatives with them that would avoid the inappropriate dual relationship.

Similarly, in case 5.3 the social worker would need to take steps to ensure that her private life, as chair of the church's capital campaign committee, would not lead to an inappropriate dual relationship with her client. The fact that the client has a history of challenges involving management of close relationships makes it especially important that the social worker establish clear boundaries. The social worker may need to discuss this issue with the client, talk about why maintaining clear boundaries is important, and recommend to the client that she consider other ways to become involved in church affairs. The social worker would need to be prepared to deal with possible clinical ramifications, for example, the possibility that the client will feel hurt and rejected.

The appropriate course of action in case 5.4 is less clear. In this instance the social worker certainly has a right to be involved in political activity. In important respects, this is an extension of her commitment to social work values related to promoting public welfare at the community and statewide levels. It would not be reasonable to expect the social worker to refrain from this kind of community and political involvement. However, the social worker should anticipate the possibility that some clients—perhaps only a few, if any—will have some feelings about the social worker's political activities and agenda. Unfortunately, some clients may have feelings about the social worker's sexual orientation. The social worker should be

117

ready to acknowledge these issues with her clients to the extent that is appropriate. Any discussion between the social worker and her clients should not promote the social worker's own personal or political agenda; rather, the focus should be exclusively on what these issues mean to the clients.

Social workers may disagree some about the extent to which their private conduct is germane to their professional work. It is difficult to prescribe strict, unambiguous criteria for determining when practitioners' private conduct interferes with their ability to perform their professional duties. As a general guide, social workers should attempt to distinguish between private conduct that directly interferes with, or has the potential to interfere with, their performance of professional functions and obligations and private conduct that is tangential or unrelated to professional obligations.

NASW *CODE OF ETHICS* STANDARDS: Commitment to Clients (1.01); Self-Determination (1.02); Conflicts of Interest (1.06); Private Conduct (4.03)

DISCUSSION QUESTIONS

1. You are a social worker in private practice. You are counseling a client who is coping with the death of her young child. The two of you have worked together for close to one year. At the end of a recent session your client told you that in the middle of the upcoming summer she would miss one of the counseling sessions; she tells you that she and her husband found out about a wonderful bed and breakfast in a neighboring state and that they would be spending a week there. Coincidentally, during each of the past six summers you and your husband and children have spent a week at the same bed and breakfast. The bed and breakfast has only five rooms; the guests gather for breakfast each morning and occasionally for dinner. You are dismayed to learn that your reservation for the upcoming summer overlaps with your client's reservation during four days. How would you handle this situation?

2. You are a social worker at a community mental health center. Your clients include people who struggle with chronic mental illness, including schizophrenia, bipolar disorder, and various anxiety disorders. One evening you are arrested by the local police and charged with driving under the influence and leaving the scene of an accident. Your arrest was publicized on local radio and television stations and in the local newspaper. Two of your clients mention the incident, which they had heard about on the news. How would you respond to the clients' comments?

Dishonesty, Fraud, and Deception

CASE 5.5. A social worker was a clinical director at a for-profit residential school for struggling teenagers. The program provided what it described as "character education" for teenagers who were not functioning well in their home communities because of various mental health, behavioral, and addiction issues. The average length of stay at the school was 15 months.

The school's staff surveyed the parents of teenagers who had graduated from the school within the past five years and asked them questions about the school's quality and effectiveness. About 40 percent of the parents returned the survey. Of these, 92 percent said they would recommend the school and 86 percent reported that their children were accepted by a college or university. Shortly after the survey results were calculated, the school stated on its Web site and printed materials that "More than 90 percent of our students' parents say that they would recommend the school to other parents, and almost 90 percent of our graduates are college students."

CASE 5.6. A social worker in private practice specialized in the counseling of trauma victims. Recently the social worker became interested in the use of a controversial form of "rebirthing therapy" for the treatment of people who experienced trauma early in their lives and who struggle with attachment issues. The social worker developed and distributed a brochure encouraging people to contact him "to discuss what this remarkably effective treatment technique can do for you!"

Discussion

Social workers are obligated to avoid any knowingly dishonest, fraudulent, or deceptive activities. Such activities not only undermine social workers' individual reputations and credibility, but also harm the entire profession's reputation and integrity.

Dishonest, fraudulent, and deceptive activities can take several forms. As in cases 5.5 and 5.6, some social workers may make exaggerated and misleading claims of effectiveness. In case 5.5, the social worker was involved in publicizing a deceptive claim that more than 90 percent of the school's students' parents say that they would recommend the school to other parents, and that almost 90 percent of the school's graduates are college students. The claim is misleading because the results are based on a limited and quite likely biased sample that only includes those parents who chose to return the survey (about 40 percent of the total that received the survey).

It is quite possible that parents who felt positively about the school were more likely to return the survey. In addition, the survey did not include parents who may have been dissatisfied with the school and withdrew their children prior to graduation or parents whose children were dismissed from the school. A similar bias could be reflected in the school's claims about its graduates' college enrollments. Furthermore, the school claimed a high percentage of college **enrollments** even though the survey only asked about college **acceptances.**

In case 5.6, the social worker made irresponsible claims about the effectiveness of rebirthing therapy. The social worker's brochure and Web site did not cite credible empirical evidence of effectiveness based on peer-reviewed, published studies that used widely respected research methodology (for example, use of representative samples, valid and reliable outcome measures and indicators, and control groups that enable researchers to rule out extraneous factors that may account for the positive results). Instead, the social worker's brochure and Web site made only broad, unsubstantiated claims that may have unduly influenced vulnerable potential clients.

Unlike blatant forms of dishonesty and deception—such as falsified records, fraudulent insurance submissions, and unsubstantiated and misleading claims of effectiveness—there are, as I discussed earlier, instances when some social workers argue that some forms of dishonesty or deception are morally justifiable because their goal is to protect vulnerable individuals. For example, social workers sometimes claim that withholding potentially traumatizing information from desperately ill clients or disturbing information from agency employees—a paternalistic form of deception—is ethically defensible. Of course, social workers' decision to be dishonest or deceptive in any form is risky and debatable.

NASW *CODE OF ETHICS* STANDARDS: Commitment to Clients (1.01); Conflicts of Interest (1.06); Consultation (2.05); Unethical Conduct of Colleagues (2.11); Dishonesty, Fraud, and Deception (4.04)

DISCUSSION QUESTIONS

1. Are there any circumstances when you think it is reasonable for social workers to be dishonest or deceptive? If you think there are exceptions, give specific examples.
2. Suppose you are an enthusiastic supporter of a cutting-edge, somewhat controversial treatment approach. You are eager to publicize the treatment approach's effectiveness. What kind of information or evidence would you need to present to avoid misleading or deceiving potential clients?

Impairment

CASE 5.7. A social worker at a family services agency provided counseling to individuals and families. He also facilitated a support group that included adolescents who had been diagnosed with ADHD (attention-deficit/hyperactivity disorder).

In his personal life, the social worker was struggling with a fragile marriage. He and his wife decided to separate. The social worker found it more and more difficult to function at work. He reported feeling depressed, admitting that he needed help.

CASE 5.8. A social work administrator was the executive director of a substance abuse treatment program that provided residential and nonresidential services. Throughout his adult life, the social worker considered himself to be a recovering alcoholic.

Recently, the chair of the agency's board of directors told the social worker that he was concerned about his behavior. According to the board chair, the social worker frequently seemed argumentative, appeared inattentive at meetings, and had been late with several important written reports submitted to the board. During an unusually frank meeting to discuss the social worker's functioning, the social worker told the board chair that "Yes, it's true that I've been slipping lately. I've been drinking socially and I know I need to put my recovery back on the front burner. I need to be a good example to everyone here."

CASE 5.9. A social worker was a unit supervisor at a juvenile correctional facility. He had worked at the institution for 22 years. During the past year the social worker grew less and less enthusiastic about his job. Frequently he called in sick. When he reported to work, the social worker found it hard to complete tasks, supervise staff under his authority, and go out of his way to help the youthful residents. The social worker was reluctant to quit his job; he wanted to hold on to qualify for the maximum pension he would receive after working for the county for 25 years. One of the social worker's colleagues expressed concern about his functioning. The social worker responded by saying, "I'll be fine. You don't need to worry about me. I have everything under control."

Discussion

In recent years social workers and other professionals have paid increased attention to the problem of impairment among practitioners. Impairment among professionals takes several forms. It may involve failure to provide competent care, failure

121

to perform one's duties, or violation of the ethical standards of the profession. By definition, impaired social workers have difficulty coping with personal stressors in their lives. Some impaired social workers, as in cases 5.7 and 5.8, are aware of and acknowledge their struggles. Some actively seek help. However, other social workers, as in case 5.9, seem unable or unwilling to acknowledge their struggles and to seek help. Often these are social workers who are genuinely "burned out."

Impairment is often a result of complex stressors in professionals' lives related to their jobs, physical health, death of a family member, marital and relationship problems, financial difficulties, midlife crises, mental illness, legal problems, and substance abuse. It is important for social workers to understand the warning signs of, and ways to prevent, impairment in their own lives. Social workers, as members of a profession that is focused on helping others, face unique challenges. Some social workers who are aware of their own impairment may not seek help because of their unwillingness to consult a colleague for assistance; their belief that they should be able to and can heal themselves; their concern about the amount of effort involved and the cost; unwillingness of a spouse or partner to participate in treatment; and their belief that professional treatment would not be effective. Recognizing these challenges, the social work profession should take assertive steps to enhance social workers' awareness of impairment risks, common warning signs, and constructive ways to respond to impairment.

NASW *Code of Ethics* standards: Commitment to Clients (1.01); Consultation (2.05); Impairment of Colleagues (2.09); Private Conduct (4.03); Impairment (4.05)

Discussion questions

1. You are the assistant director of a mental health center. You want to devote a staff meeting to the subject of impaired professionals. What information would you include in this presentation?

2. What specific steps can the social work profession take to educate practitioners about professional impairment?

Misrepresentation

Case 5.10. A social worker was the executive director of a statewide social welfare association. The organization had 1,700 members; the social worker was responsible for administering the office, organizing conferences and continuing education, serving as a liaison with other professional associations, and lobbying public officials on behalf of the association.

In her private life the social worker was very involved in abortion rights advocacy. Often she attended rallies and got involved in public education campaigns. At one highly publicized event at the state house that protested the governor's veto of an abortion rights bill, the social worker spoke to the large crowd and identified herself as the executive director of the statewide social welfare association.

CASE 5.11. A social worker resigned his position at a mental health center to start a private practice. Before he became a social worker, the man had been a biochemist for 15 years. He had earned a PhD in biochemistry before embarking on his second career as a social worker.

The social worker was eager to build his private practice. In his promotional material he referred to himself as "Doctor," using the title with which he was addressed during his career as a biochemist.

Discussion

By virtue of their professional education and expertise, social workers are often in a position to present themselves as experts and express authoritative opinions. They may be consulted by the media, speak at professional conferences, or consult with colleagues and members of the public. Social workers who present themselves as experts and express authoritative opinions must be careful to distinguish between statements they make and activities they become involved in as private citizens and as members of the social work profession. They must be certain to avoid misrepresenting their affiliation and creating misleading impressions about whom they represent. In case 5.10, the social worker certainly had the right to become involved in advocacy and political activity that reflect her personal values. However, she should not have linked her widely publicized statements and advocacy with her official position as executive director of a statewide social welfare association, unless her organization had taken an official position on this issue and authorized the social worker to speak on its behalf. Doing so likely created the public perception that her views and activities reflected the opinions and priorities of the association's members.

Furthermore, social workers should not mislead clients, potential clients, the public at large, colleagues, or employers about their educational credentials, professional experience, expertise, and background. Social workers should not exaggerate or embellish their qualifications, and they should be sure to correct any inaccuracies or misrepresentations of their credentials. Thus, the social worker in case 5.11 should not use the title "Doctor" in material and advertisements promoting his private practice. The average potential client would likely conclude that the social worker has a doctorate that is directly relevant to mental health counseling. Some potential clients' choice of practitioner may be influenced by their perception that the practitioner has doctoral-level education. The fact that the social worker's doctorate is in biochemistry would misrepresent his social work–related expertise and would be misleading.

NASW *Code of Ethics* standards: Commitment to Clients (1.01); Conflicts of Interest (1.06); Commitments to Employers (3.09); Private Conduct (4.03); Misrepresentation (4.06)

Discussion questions

1. You are a recent MSW recipient and have accepted a position as a counselor at a family services agency. Before attending social work graduate school, you were a practicing lawyer. As a law school graduate and practicing lawyer you used the initials JD (meaning Juris Doctor) following your name. In your job as a counselor, should you identify yourself as MSW, JD on your business cards and when you sign letters and documents?

2. You are a social worker who is employed at a counseling center. You also attended a training institute and obtained your license as a massage therapist. On weekends you have a part-time massage practice. Many of your massage clients talk about personal issues during massages. You wonder whether you should list your MSW on your brochure promoting your massage practice along with your LMT (licensed massage therapist) credential. What are the arguments for and against?

Solicitations

CASE 5.12. A social worker in private practice got a telephone call from a colleague who consults with a local police department. The colleague asked the social worker if he would help provide crisis intervention services to hundreds of people who lost their homes during a recent hurricane. The social worker met with dozens of people who were staying in a local school's gymnasium and at area hotels. At the conclusion of each meeting, the social worker handed the people his business (private practice) card and invited them to contact him if they needed additional help.

CASE 5.13. A social worker was the clinical director of a substance abuse treatment center. The social worker was a member of a committee at the agency that was putting together a public relations and marketing strategy to enhance the treatment center's visibility in the local community. The treatment center's assistant director asked the social worker to identify "three or four of our most satisfied former residents who might be willing to appear in commercials and print advertisements" publicizing the program.

Discussion

Social workers are certainly free to publicize their services. However, social workers should not actively reach out and solicit clients among people who, because of their traumatic circumstances, may be vulnerable to pressure, subtle or otherwise. In case 5.12, the people who were displaced by the hurricane clearly were in a vulnerable position. It would be commendable of the social worker to offer his pro bono services to help people who were coping with tremendous loss. But a social worker in this kind of situation should not take advantage of such a predicament to solicit new clients. At the very least, this has the appearance of impropriety. It can also constitute an unconscionable form of undue influence.

Social workers also have to be careful about soliciting client testimonials. Certainly social workers should never ask a current client for a testimonial about the social worker's skill or the quality of a program or service. Current clients may experience being asked for this kind of endorsement as coercive, manipulative, or exploitative, and they may feel obligated to consent to the request to avoid jeopardizing their receipt of services or their relationship with their service provider.

Social workers also must be careful not to exploit or coerce former clients. Some former clients may be quite vulnerable and susceptible to undue influence. In case 5.13, some of the former clients the social worker might approach for a testimonial may feel indebted to their social worker or to the treatment center and might feel obligated to consent to the request. Former clients who feel pressured or obligated to cooperate may end up feeling overexposed by the publicity and may feel as if their privacy has been invaded. Although former clients have the right to consent, there is always a risk that their consent would not satisfy the criteria for truly voluntary, informed consent.

NASW *Code of Ethics* standards: Commitment to Clients (1.01); Informed Consent (1.03); Conflicts of Interest (1.06); Consultation (2.05); Administration (3.07); Commitments to Employers (3.09); Solicitations (4.07)

Discussion questions

1. You are a social worker who is building a private practice. Under what circumstances, if any, would it be permissible for you to solicit new clients? What guidelines should govern social workers' solicitation of clients?

2. Under what circumstances, if any, is it permissible for social workers to publicize testimonial endorsements provided by former clients? What guidelines should govern social workers' use of former clients' testimonials?

Acknowledging Credit

Case 5.13. A team of social workers in a hospital-based treatment program for adolescents with eating disorders developed an empirically based treatment model based on a combination of cognitive–behavioral intervention and family counseling. The team wrote a detailed treatment manual for publication by a major publisher. When the team leader informed the agency director— who was also a social worker—of their plans, the director insisted that his name appear on the list of authors. The staffers who had developed the model and written the manual felt exploited by the agency director, who had not been involved in the treatment model's development.

Case 5.14. A social worker was employed by a child welfare research institute affiliated with a graduate school of social work. She was the director of a federally funded research project that assessed the impact of long-term foster care on foster children and foster parents. The social worker and her staff, including two research assistants who were doctoral students at the school, gathered extensive data by interviewing foster children and foster parents. The research staff also gathered data from records maintained by area juvenile courts and police departments.

Once the data were analyzed, the social worker in charge of the project prepared several research reports and manuscripts that she submitted to professional journals for possible publication. Three manuscripts were published. The two research assistants, who contributed a great deal to the research project and manuscript preparation, were dismayed when they discovered that the project director listed only herself as the author and did not acknowledge the research assistants' significant contributions.

Discussion

It is important for social workers to treat colleagues fairly and with integrity. Social workers should not claim to have performed work that they did not actually do, as in case 5.13. This includes work on research projects, program development, grant applications, and other professional endeavors. Social workers should take responsibility and credit that is in direct proportion to the work they have actually performed or to which they have contributed. It was not appropriate for the agency director to insert his name as a coauthor when he had not contributed at all to the written publication. If the authors wished, they could include a footnote acknowledging the agency director's support of the project.

The circumstances in case 5.14 are the reverse, in that the efforts of staffers who contributed significantly to a project were not acknowledged by the project director. Social workers who have received assistance from others in activities such as research, project development, and program administration always should give credit where it is due. The project director in case 5.14 should have acknowledged the substantial contributions of the doctoral students who served as research assistants.

In addition, social workers should always cite the work of others on which they draw when preparing written or electronic (Web site) reports, whether published or unpublished. Social workers who prepare written documents should always accurately cite all of their sources. Social workers should not take credit for ideas that are not their own and must not plagiarize the work of others.

NASW *Code of Ethics* standards: Respect (2.01); Unethical Conduct of Colleagues (2.11); Administration (3.07); Dishonesty, Fraud, and Deception (4.04); Acknowledging Credit (4.08)

Discussion questions
1. You are the director of a large research project studying the effectiveness of a respite program for family members who care for a relative with severe dementia. The research project includes extensive interviews with family members about stressors in their lives and the strengths and limitations of the respite program. You supervise six social work students who conduct interviews, collate the data, and create computer-based data files. Two of the students assisted with data analysis and interpretation and helped out with early drafts of research reports. What guidelines and criteria would you use to acknowledge the contributions of the research project staffers?

2. You are the clinical director of a program that provides counseling services and crisis intervention for gay, lesbian, bisexual, and transgender adolescents. You and your colleagues attend a national conference on an innovative suicide prevention protocol that can be used with this client population. After the conference you contact the presenter, who works in another state, and ask her if she would be willing to share a copy of their program's detailed written description of the program model, clinical protocol, and training curriculum. The presenter sends you the materials; you review them and are extremely impressed. You would like to use the materials and framework in your own agency. What steps would you take before using the materials included in the conference presentation and in the written materials?

chapter six

Ethical Responsibilities to the Social Work Profession and the Broader Society

Social workers' ethical duties extend beyond their commitment to clients and colleagues. They also include responsibilities to the social work profession itself and the broader society.

Integrity of the Profession

CASE 6.1. An unlicensed counselor provided "holistic" healing services. These services included body work, energy healing, trigger point therapy, and chakra alignment. The counselor was eager to be eligible for insurance reimbursement. She consulted with several colleagues who advised her to obtain her MSW so that she could become a licensed mental health provider. The counselor enrolled in a local MSW program but claimed to have no interest in social work as a profession. She confided to one student, "I'm just putting in my time here so I can get the degree and apply for licensure. I couldn't care less about most of this stuff concerning social work values, social work history, social policy, and all that."

CASE 6.2. A social worker was a program director in a vocational education program for people with physical and cognitive disabilities. The program offered mental health counseling to the program's clients. Recently, one of the social worker's colleagues at the agency, a vocational counselor, started to spend half of her time in the program's mental health unit. The social worker learned that her colleague had a master's in education, specializing in vocational counseling, but was not a licensed mental health counselor. However, the colleague signed her progress notes using the title "social worker" when she worked with clients in the mental health unit.

Discussion

Ideally, people choose to become social workers because they identify with the profession's unique values and mission. Although some social work functions and intervention models share features with other helping professions—such as counseling, psychology, pastoral counseling, and public administration—social work clearly has unique historical roots and a corpus of unique values, conceptual frameworks, theories, and intervention approaches.

Occasionally, as in case 6.1, people will enroll in a social work education program because it is the "path of least resistance" or because it is the fastest and most efficient path to licensure and insurance reimbursement. Over time, some of these people come to appreciate what it means to be a social worker and gradually embrace this professional identity. However, some of these students never fully embrace social work's values and mission and, after graduation, may not identify or refer to themselves as social workers. Rather, they consider themselves to be therapists, counselors, or healers.

Although it is important for social workers to identify with and promote the profession, it is perfectly appropriate for social workers to engage in responsible criticism of the profession. Ultimately the profession is strengthened when its members continually monitor, examine, and, when appropriate, critique prevailing standards, practices, policy statements, and ideological positions. As in all professions, over time values, priorities, and opinions on key issues may need to change as compelling societal events occur and trends develop. For example, the remarkable advent of sophisticated ways for social workers to communicate electronically—via e-mail, text messaging, blogs, and fax machines—has forced the profession to develop new ethical standards regarding protection of client privacy and confidentiality. Similarly, stunning medical developments have required social workers in health care settings to adjust their ethics-related thinking about end-of-life care, patients' right to refuse treatment, and the allocation of scarce health care resources.

Social work should be practiced only by people who have proper education and training and who possess the competencies, licenses, and credentials required for their particular positions and areas of practice. Unauthorized or unqualified social work practice can occur in several ways. As in case 6.2, some individuals without formal social work education present themselves as social work professionals. Also, some individuals claim qualifications and expertise they do not have. These individuals may advertise skills and knowledge they do not possess—such as clinical expertise or research or administration skills—in an effort to gain employment, solicit clients, and attract funding. In other instances, social workers hire unlicensed and unqualified employees to provide services. Social workers who use assistants in this way misrepresent their expertise and services.

NASW *Code of Ethics* standards: Commitment to Clients (1.01); Competence (1.04 and 4.01); Unethical Conduct of Colleagues (2.11); Dishonesty, Fraud, and Deception (4.04); Misrepresentation (4.06); Integrity of the Profession (5.01)

Discussion questions
1. You are the director of admissions at a graduate school of social work. You oversee the admissions process for people who apply to your school's MSW program. What steps would you take to enhance the likelihood that students who enroll in your school are committed to the social work profession?
2. What laws or regulations exist in your state concerning the use of the title "social worker"? Who is permitted to use this title? What qualifications do they have to meet?

Evaluation and Research

Case 6.3. A social work graduate student needed to complete a year-long research and evaluation project in the final year of her program. The student designed a study that involved interviewing older adolescents who do not have families and reside in an independent living program that helps the teenagers gain the knowledge and skills they will need to live on their own. The student developed a sampling strategy, data collection instruments, and began conducting in-depth interviews.

The social work student explained the research project to each eligible teenager and obtained their approval. During one interview, the teenager began crying uncontrollably as he talked about how he was physically and sexually abused as a child by his stepfather. The student did her best to comfort the teenager. The student was eager to complete the interview, which was essential to completing her school's graduation requirements.

Case 6.4. A social worker was the research director at a psychiatric hospital affiliated with a major university medical center. The social worker supervised a federally funded research project designed to evaluate the effectiveness of a treatment model for people with co-occurring symptoms and dual diagnoses involving major mental illness and substance abuse. As part of the research project, clients received weekly counseling, psychotropic medication, and emergency services. Clients were interviewed about their symptoms and challenges and their experiences in the program; they also completed several standardized instruments that measure aspects of their mental health and substance abuse.

One afternoon, the social worker was visited by a police detective. The detective explained that she was investigating a recent rape; she told the social worker that the police had received a tip that the suspect was enrolled in the hospital's research project. The detective showed the social worker a photograph of one of the research project's participants and asked the social worker whether she recognized the man in the photo. The social worker was unsure about whether to acknowledge that the man is a participant in the hospital's research project.

CASE 6.5. A social work professor was conducting a long-term study of the effectiveness of different types of marriage and couple's counseling. As part of the research project, couples involved in counseling were interviewed about their experiences with, and the effectiveness of, the treatment they have received. The in-depth interviews addressed very personal, intimate information about the participants' lives. Couples who participated in the project were referred to the social work professor by clinicians in the local area.

In the middle of one of the interviews, which were conducted during the summer months, the professor discovered that the wife he was interviewing would be the professor's child's high school English teacher when the school year started in 3 weeks. The professor was unsure about whether to complete the interview.

Discussion

It is vitally important for social workers to monitor and evaluate clinical intervention, community organizing, policy implementation, and agency administration. Data obtained from well-designed research and evaluation are critical to effective and ethical practice. Furthermore, social workers are increasingly aware that practitioners have an ethical responsibility to base their practice on empirical evidence of effectiveness.

Standards to ensure that research and evaluation are conducted ethically and to protect research and evaluation participants have matured considerably, especially since the mid-20th century. Contemporary social work research and evaluation must comply with key ethics standards that ensure that participants are not coerced and fully consent; participants are mentally competent to provide informed consent; and participants have the right to refuse or withdraw consent.

In general, two groups of people may be unable to provide informed consent to participate in research and evaluation: children and people who do not have the mental competence to consent. When evaluation and research participants lack the capacity to provide informed consent, social workers should protect them by seeking written permission from an appropriate third party (for example, parent, guardian, or legal representative). In such instances, social work researchers should ensure that the proxy acts in a manner consistent with participants' wishes and interests. In case 6.3, for example, the research sample included teenagers who, legally, are not authorized to provide informed consent. The social worker student would need to obtain consent from individuals who are authorized to consent on the teenagers' behalf (for example, a legal guardian or public child welfare official). Even though the teenagers would not be in a position to provide the social work student with legally valid **consent**, the student should seek the teenagers' **assent** in an effort to acknowledge and respect their wishes.

On occasion, social workers may not be able to obtain, or would not be expected to obtain, participants' informed consent. For example, this can occur when social workers observe the behavior of people who are in public settings, such as the choices some homeless people make to sleep under bridges, in alleys, or over heating grates in public walkways.

Sometimes social workers discover that evaluation and research participants need supportive or crisis services, as in case 6.3. In these instances, social workers are ethically obligated to take reasonable steps to assess clients' needs and refer them for appropriate services. Completion of the research or data-gathering task would be secondary. Social workers' first priority must be protecting participants from unwarranted mental or physical distress and harm.

As in case 6.4, social workers involved in research and evaluation sometimes encounter complex ethical dilemmas related to the confidentiality of the data they collect. In general, social workers should protect research data in the way they protect clinical or other confidential information. This information should not be disclosed unless disclosure is required under the handful of well-known exceptions to clients' right to confidentiality, for example, to prevent harm to the research participant or others (where there is evidence of serious, foreseeable, and imminent harm); to comply with mandatory reporting requirements; or in response to a court order. Social work researchers should always be mindful of relevant NASW *Code of Ethics* standards and relevant federal and state laws (for example, strict guidelines concerning the protection of confidential information related to substance abuse assessment and treatment, mandatory reporting, treatment of minors and school children, and protected health information). In case 6.4, for example, federal law would likely prohibit the social work researcher's disclosure of confidential information in the absence of a court order that was signed by a judge who reviewed the police department's request for confidential information related to substance abuse treatment and who considered whether there was a compelling reason for the disclosure without the research participant's consent.

Social work evaluators and researchers must be careful to avoid conflicts of interest and problematic dual relationships with participants when there is a risk of exploitation of potential harm to the participants. In case 6.5, for example, the woman interviewed by the social work professor—who was scheduled to become the professor's child's high school English teacher—might feel overexposed and vulnerable as a result of sharing such intimate information with the parent of one of her students. This dual relationship could also inadvertently affect the teacher's relationship with the social work professor's son, in that she might feel the need to distance herself from him in a way that is out of the ordinary. Furthermore, the teacher's and father's willingness to approach each other, if necessary, during the course of the school year concerning the child's school performance could be negatively affected.

When possible, social work researchers and evaluators should always inform participants when a real or potential conflict of interest arises. Social workers should always take steps to resolve the issue in a manner that makes the participants' interests primary.

NASW *Code of Ethics* standards: Commitment to Clients (1.01); Informed Consent (1.03); Conflicts of Interest (1.06); Clients Who Lack Decision-Making Capacity (1.14); Consultation (2.05); Integrity of the Profession (5.01); Evaluation and Research (5.02)

Discussion questions

1. You are a social work student who is taking an advanced research and evaluation course. One of the course requirements is to design and conduct a research and evaluation project. Your project involves interviewing residents of a juvenile detention facility about their mental health needs. Your goal is to assess the adequacy of mental health services available to this client

population in light of their needs. What steps would you take to ensure compliance with ethical standards related to research and evaluation?

2. One morning a police detective contacts you and explains that she knows that you have been conducting in-depth interviews with the juvenile detention center's residents about their involvement in violent behavior (the detective learned this from the center's administrator, who was asked to list all staffers who have access to information about the residents). The detective explains to you that she is conducting an investigation of allegations that one of the youths you interviewed stabbed a neighborhood girl. The detective wants to know whether the resident mentioned anything to you about this incident. How would you respond?

Social Welfare

Case 6.6. A social worker in a state department of human services provided casework services to low-income people who are in dire financial straits. Most of the social worker's clients were single parents with children.

At an afternoon staff meeting the social worker learned that the governor and the department's director had just issued a joint order drastically reducing benefits, tightening eligibility criteria, and shortening the length of time clients are eligible to receive benefits.

The social worker was distressed about the likely impact of these changes on vulnerable clients. She was convinced that wasteful spending elsewhere in the department should be curtailed before implementing the proposed cuts. The social worker met informally with several colleagues who shared her concerns and discussed steps they might take to raise public awareness and challenge the proposal's provisions.

Case 6.7. A social worker in private practice turned on the local news and learned of a shooting at a local middle school. According to the broadcast, a student who had been suspended from the school returned with a gun, forced his way into the building through a side door, and began shooting randomly in a crowded hallway. Four students, one teacher, and a school custodian were murdered; many other students and staffers were injured. The city's mayor announced that all uninjured students and personnel would be sent home as soon as safe conditions were restored.

Shortly after the broadcast the social worker received an e-mail alert from the executive director of the state's NASW chapter inviting social work clinicians who were experienced in crisis intervention and trauma work to contact her about volunteering during the next few days to help surviving students, staffers, and family members. The social worker looked at her schedule, which was jam-packed with nearly back-to-back appointments. The social worker was concerned about cancelling clients and losing much needed income. Yet, the social worker was also eager to help out local citizens in need.

Discussion

One of social work's distinguishing features is the profession's enduring commitment to social welfare and the broader society. Social work's history is anchored in concern about the commonwealth in addition to concern about individuals. Social workers understand that people's problems—poverty, substance abuse, mental illness, and so on—are often a function of cultural, social, and environmental forces, as well as individual dynamics. Social workers also know that in many cases the most effective way to prevent individual suffering is to address influential social policies.

Social workers can take steps to facilitate and promote public participation by educating the public about important social concerns. Social workers can sponsor and participate in educational forums, workshops, and lectures. They can also offer to consult with media outlets about pressing social and public policy issues. Many social workers become involved in efforts to organize clients and community groups to influence agency administrators, legislators, and other public officials who are responsible for designing and administering social policies. In case 6.6, the social worker could take assertive steps to educate and organize colleagues and members of the public about the needs of low-income, vulnerable people and explore reasonable and realistic policy options. Of course, the fact that the social worker is an employee of the state agency that is affected by the governor's and department director's order may limit her ability to advocate publicly, but she may be able to participate in a number of educational and advocacy activities without jeopardizing her job or violating any regulations.

Social workers also have a responsibility, when feasible, to provide assistance to people and communities affected by public emergencies, as in case 6.7. This kind of assistance is consistent with the ethical principle articulated in the NASW *Code of Ethics* that states, "Social workers are encouraged to volunteer some portion of their professional skills with no expectation of significant financial return (pro bono service)." Whenever possible, and when such service would not impose an unreasonable burden on practitioners, social workers should offer their professional services in local, national, and international crises to victims and surviving relatives and loved ones. Depending on their educational training and experience, social workers may be in a position to provide counseling and casework services, organize communities, and plan the delivery of services.

The expectation that social workers will provide assistance during public emergencies must be tempered with a realistic understanding of the practical limitations most professionals face with respect to the time and energy available for such pro bono assistance. Social workers have limited financial and other resources and must make difficult judgments about which professional and personal obligations in their lives should take precedence. What is important is for social workers to recognize this ethical ideal and do what they can to meet it.

NASW *Code of Ethics* standards: Commitment to Clients (1.01); Integrity of the Profession (5.01); Social Welfare (6.01); Public Participation (6.02); Public Emergencies (6.03); Social and Political Action (6.04)

Discussion questions

1. You are a social worker who administers a community action program that offers emergency food, shelter, and clothing to people in need. About 30 percent of your agency's budget comes from city funds. You were just informed that the mayor has ordered all agencies that receive city funds to verify that people who seek services are U.S. citizens. The mayor announced in a press conference that the city can no longer afford to assist undocumented immigrants. How would you respond to this order? What steps, if any, would you take to address the potential impact of the mayor's order?

2. You are a social worker in private practice. You feel strongly about devoting a portion of your time to public service, especially during public emergencies. How would you go about deciding how much time to devote to public service? What would your personal policy be?

NASW *Code of Ethics**

Preamble

The primary mission of the social work profession is to enhance human well-being and help meet the basic human needs of all people, with particular attention to the needs and empowerment of people who are vulnerable, oppressed, and living in poverty. A historic and defining feature of social work is the profession's focus on individual well-being in a social context and the well-being of society. Fundamental to social work is attention to the environmental forces that create, contribute to, and address problems in living.

Social workers promote social justice and social change with and on behalf of clients. "Clients" is used inclusively to refer to individuals, families, groups, organizations, and communities. Social workers are sensitive to cultural and ethnic diversity and strive to end discrimination, oppression, poverty, and other forms of social injustice. These activities may be in the form of direct practice, community organizing, supervision, consultation, administration, advocacy, social and political action, policy development and implementation, education, and research and evaluation. Social workers seek to enhance the capacity of people to address their own needs. Social workers also seek to promote the responsiveness of organizations, communities, and other social institutions to individuals' needs and social problems.

The mission of the social work profession is rooted in a set of core values. These core values, embraced by social workers throughout the profession's history, are the foundation of social work's unique purpose and perspective:

---

*Approved by the 1996 NASW Delegate Assembly and revised by the 1999 NASW Delegate Assembly.

- ◆ service
- ◆ social justice
- ◆ dignity and worth of the person
- ◆ importance of human relationships
- ◆ integrity
- ◆ competence.

This constellation of core values reflects what is unique to the social work profession. Core values, and the principles that flow from them, must be balanced within the context and complexity of the human experience.

Purpose of the NASW Code of Ethics

Professional ethics are at the core of social work. The profession has an obligation to articulate its basic values, ethical principles, and ethical standards. The *NASW Code of Ethics* sets forth these values, principles, and standards to guide social workers' conduct. The *Code* is relevant to all social workers and social work students, regardless of their professional functions, the settings in which they work, or the populations they serve.

The *NASW Code of Ethics* serves six purposes:

1. The *Code* identifies core values on which social work's mission is based.
2. The *Code* summarizes broad ethical principles that reflect the profession's core values and establishes a set of specific ethical standards that should be used to guide social work practice.
3. The *Code* is designed to help social workers identify relevant considerations when professional obligations conflict or ethical uncertainties arise.
4. The *Code* provides ethical standards to which the general public can hold the social work profession accountable.
5. The *Code* socializes practitioners new to the field to social work's mission, values, ethical principles, and ethical standards.
6. The *Code* articulates standards that the social work profession itself can use to assess whether social workers have engaged in unethical conduct. NASW has formal procedures to adjudicate ethics complaints filed against its members.[1] In subscribing to this *Code*, social workers are required to cooperate

---

1. For information on NASW adjudication procedures, see *NASW Procedures for the Adjudication of Grievances*.

in its implementation, participate in NASW adjudication proceedings, and abide by any NASW disciplinary rulings or sanctions based on it.

The *Code* offers a set of values, principles, and standards to guide decision making and conduct when ethical issues arise. It does not provide a set of rules that prescribe how social workers should act in all situations. Specific applications of the *Code* must take into account the context in which it is being considered and the possibility of conflicts among the *Code's* values, principles, and standards. Ethical responsibilities flow from all human relationships, from the personal and familial to the social and professional.

Further, the *NASW Code of Ethics* does not specify which values, principles, and standards are most important and ought to outweigh others in instances when they conflict. Reasonable differences of opinion can and do exist among social workers with respect to the ways in which values, ethical principles, and ethical standards should be rank ordered when they conflict. Ethical decision making in a given situation must apply the informed judgment of the individual social worker and should also consider how the issues would be judged in a peer review process where the ethical standards of the profession would be applied.

Ethical decision making is a process. There are many instances in social work where simple answers are not available to resolve complex ethical issues. Social workers should take into consideration all the values, principles, and standards in this *Code* that are relevant to any situation in which ethical judgment is warranted. Social workers' decisions and actions should be consistent with the spirit as well as the letter of this *Code*.

In addition to this *Code*, there are many other sources of information about ethical thinking that may be useful. Social workers should consider ethical theory and principles generally, social work theory and research, laws, regulations, agency policies, and other relevant codes of ethics, recognizing that among codes of ethics, social workers should consider the *NASW Code of Ethics* as their primary source. Social workers also should be aware of the impact on ethical decision making of their clients' and their own personal values and cultural and religious beliefs and practices. They should be aware of any conflicts between personal and professional values and deal with them responsibly. For additional guidance social workers should consult the relevant literature on professional ethics and ethical decision making and seek appropriate consultation when faced with ethical dilemmas. This may involve consultation with an agency-based or social work organization's ethics committee, a regulatory body, knowledgeable colleagues, supervisors, or legal counsel.

Instances may arise when social workers' ethical obligations conflict with agency policies or relevant laws or regulations. When such conflicts occur, social workers must make a responsible effort to resolve the conflict in a manner that is consistent with the values, principles, and standards expressed in this *Code*. If a reasonable resolution of the conflict does not appear possible, social workers should seek proper consultation before making a decision.

The *NASW Code of Ethics* is to be used by NASW and by individuals, agencies, organizations, and bodies (such as licensing and regulatory boards, professional liability insurance providers, courts of law, agency boards of directors, government agencies, and other professional groups) that choose to adopt it or use it as a frame of reference. Violation of standards in this *Code* does not automatically imply legal liability or violation of the law. Such determination can only be made in the context of legal and judicial proceedings. Alleged violations of the *Code* would be subject to a peer review process. Such processes are generally separate from legal or administrative procedures and insulated from legal review or proceedings to allow the profession to counsel and discipline its own members.

A code of ethics cannot guarantee ethical behavior. Moreover, a code of ethics cannot resolve all ethical issues or disputes or capture the richness and complexity involved in striving to make responsible choices within a moral community. Rather, a code of ethics sets forth values, ethical principles, and ethical standards to which professionals aspire and by which their actions can be judged. Social workers' ethical behavior should result from their personal commitment to engage in ethical practice. The *NASW Code of Ethics* reflects the commitment of all social workers to uphold the profession's values and to act ethically. Principles and standards must be applied by individuals of good character who discern moral questions and, in good faith, seek to make reliable ethical judgments.

Ethical Principles

The following broad ethical principles are based on social work's core values of service, social justice, dignity and worth of the person, importance of human relationships, integrity, and competence. These principles set forth ideals to which all social workers should aspire.

Value: *Service*
Ethical Principle: *Social workers' primary goal is to help people in need and to address social problems.*

142

Social workers elevate service to others above self-interest. Social workers draw on their knowledge, values, and skills to help people in need and to address social problems. Social workers are encouraged to volunteer some portion of their professional skills with no expectation of significant financial return (pro bono service).

Value: *Social Justice*
Ethical Principle: *Social workers challenge social injustice.*
Social workers pursue social change, particularly with and on behalf of vulnerable and oppressed individuals and groups of people. Social workers' social change efforts are focused primarily on issues of poverty, unemployment, discrimination, and other forms of social injustice. These activities seek to promote sensitivity to and knowledge about oppression and cultural and ethnic diversity. Social workers strive to ensure access to needed information, services, and resources; equality of opportunity; and meaningful participation in decision making for all people.

Value: *Dignity and Worth of the Person*
Ethical Principle: *Social workers respect the inherent dignity and worth of the person.*
Social workers treat each person in a caring and respectful fashion, mindful of individual differences and cultural and ethnic diversity. Social workers promote clients' socially responsible self-determination. Social workers seek to enhance clients' capacity and opportunity to change and to address their own needs. Social workers are cognizant of their dual responsibility to clients and to the broader society. They seek to resolve conflicts between clients' interests and the broader society's interests in a socially responsible manner consistent with the values, ethical principles, and ethical standards of the profession.

Value: *Importance of Human Relationships*
Ethical Principle: *Social workers recognize the central importance of human relationships.*
Social workers understand that relationships between and among people are an important vehicle for change. Social workers engage people as partners in the helping process. Social workers seek to strengthen relationships among people in a purposeful effort to promote, restore, maintain, and enhance the well-being of individuals, families, social groups, organizations, and communities.

Value: *Integrity*
Ethical Principle: *Social workers behave in a trustworthy manner.*
Social workers are continually aware of the profession's mission, values, ethical principles, and ethical standards and practice in a manner consistent with them. Social

workers act honestly and responsibly and promote ethical practices on the part of the organizations with which they are affiliated.

Value: *Competence*
Ethical Principle: *Social workers practice within their areas of competence and develop and enhance their professional expertise.*
Social workers continually strive to increase their professional knowledge and skills and to apply them in practice. Social workers should aspire to contribute to the knowledge base of the profession.

Ethical Standards

The following ethical standards are relevant to the professional activities of all social workers. These standards concern (1) social workers' ethical responsibilities to clients, (2) social workers' ethical responsibilities to colleagues, (3) social workers' ethical responsibilities in practice settings, (4) social workers' ethical responsibilities as professionals, (5) social workers' ethical responsibilities to the social work profession, and (6) social workers' ethical responsibilities to the broader society.

Some of the standards that follow are enforceable guidelines for professional conduct, and some are aspirational. The extent to which each standard is enforceable is a matter of professional judgment to be exercised by those responsible for reviewing alleged violations of ethical standards.

1. **Social Workers' Ethical Responsibilities to Clients**
   1.01 Commitment to Clients
   Social workers' primary responsibility is to promote the well-being of clients. In general, clients' interests are primary. However, social workers' responsibility to the larger society or specific legal obligations may on limited occasions supersede the loyalty owed clients, and clients should be so advised. (Examples include when a social worker is required by law to report that a client has abused a child or has threatened to harm self or others.)

   1.02 Self-Determination
   Social workers respect and promote the right of clients to self-determination and assist clients in their efforts to identify and clarify their goals. Social workers may limit clients' right to self-determination when, in the social workers' professional judgment, clients' actions or potential actions pose a serious, foreseeable, and imminent risk to themselves or others.

1.03 Informed Consent

(a) Social workers should provide services to clients only in the context of a professional relationship based, when appropriate, on valid informed consent. Social workers should use clear and understandable language to inform clients of the purpose of the services, risks related to the services, limits to services because of the requirements of a third-party payer, relevant costs, reasonable alternatives, clients' right to refuse or withdraw consent, and the time frame covered by the consent. Social workers should provide clients with an opportunity to ask questions.

(b) In instances when clients are not literate or have difficulty understanding the primary language used in the practice setting, social workers should take steps to ensure clients' comprehension. This may include providing clients with a detailed verbal explanation or arranging for a qualified interpreter or translator whenever possible.

(c) In instances when clients lack the capacity to provide informed consent, social workers should protect clients' interests by seeking permission from an appropriate third party, informing clients consistent with the clients' level of understanding. In such instances social workers should seek to ensure that the third party acts in a manner consistent with clients' wishes and interests. Social workers should take reasonable steps to enhance such clients' ability to give informed consent.

(d) In instances when clients are receiving services involuntarily, social workers should provide information about the nature and extent of services and about the extent of clients' right to refuse service.

(e) Social workers who provide services via electronic media (such as computer, telephone, radio, and television) should inform recipients of the limitations and risks associated with such services.

(f) Social workers should obtain clients' informed consent before audiotaping or videotaping clients or permitting observation of services to clients by a third party.

1.04 Competence

(a) Social workers should provide services and represent themselves as competent only within the boundaries of their education, training, license, certification, consultation received, supervised experience, or other relevant professional experience.

(b) Social workers should provide services in substantive areas or use intervention techniques or approaches that are new to them only after engaging in appropriate study, training, consultation, and supervision from people who are competent in those interventions or techniques.

(c) When generally recognized standards do not exist with respect to an emerging area of practice, social workers should exercise careful judgment and take responsible steps (including appropriate education, research, training, consultation, and supervision) to ensure the competence of their work and to protect clients from harm.

1.05 Cultural Competence and Social Diversity

(a) Social workers should understand culture and its function in human behavior and society, recognizing the strengths that exist in all cultures.

(b) Social workers should have a knowledge base of their clients' cultures and be able to demonstrate competence in the provision of services that are sensitive to clients' cultures and to differences among people and cultural groups.

(c) Social workers should obtain education about and seek to understand the nature of social diversity and oppression with respect to race, ethnicity, national origin, color, sex, sexual orientation, age, marital status, political belief, religion, and mental or physical disability.

1.06 Conflicts of Interest

(a) Social workers should be alert to and avoid conflicts of interest that interfere with the exercise of professional discretion and impartial judgment. Social workers should inform clients when a real or potential conflict of interest arises and take reasonable steps to resolve the issue in a manner that makes the clients' interests primary and protects clients' interests to the greatest extent possible. In some cases, protecting clients' interests may require termination of the professional relationship with proper referral of the client.

(b) Social workers should not take unfair advantage of any professional relationship or exploit others to further their personal, religious, political, or business interests.

(c) Social workers should not engage in dual or multiple relationships with clients or former clients in which there is a risk of exploitation or potential harm to the client. In instances when dual or multiple relationships are unavoidable, social workers should take steps to protect clients and are responsible for setting clear, appropriate, and culturally sensitive boundaries. (Dual or multiple relationships occur when social workers relate to clients in more than one relationship, whether professional, social, or business. Dual or multiple relationships can occur simultaneously or consecutively.)

(d) When social workers provide services to two or more people who have a relationship with each other (for example, couples, family members), social workers should clarify with all parties which individuals will be considered clients and the nature of social workers' professional obligations to the various individuals who are receiving services. Social workers who anticipate a conflict of interest among the individuals receiving services or who anticipate having to perform in potentially conflicting roles (for example, when a social worker is asked to testify in a child custody dispute or divorce proceedings involving clients) should clarify their role with the parties involved and take appropriate action to minimize any conflict of interest.

1.07 Privacy and Confidentiality

(a) Social workers should respect clients' right to privacy. Social workers should not solicit private information from clients unless it is essential to providing services or conducting social work evaluation or research. Once private information is shared, standards of confidentiality apply.

(b) Social workers may disclose confidential information when appropriate with valid consent from a client or a person legally authorized to consent on behalf of a client.

(c) Social workers should protect the confidentiality of all information obtained in the course of professional service, except for compelling professional reasons. The general expectation that social workers will keep information confidential does not apply when disclosure is necessary to prevent serious, foreseeable, and imminent harm to a client or other identifiable person. In all instances, social workers should disclose the least amount of confidential information necessary to achieve the desired purpose; only information that is directly relevant to the purpose for which the disclosure is made should be revealed.

(d) Social workers should inform clients, to the extent possible, about the disclosure of confidential information and the potential consequences, when feasible before the disclosure is made. This applies whether social workers disclose confidential information on the basis of a legal requirement or client consent.

(e) Social workers should discuss with clients and other interested parties the nature of confidentiality and limitations of clients' right to confidentiality. Social workers should review with clients circumstances where confidential information may be requested and where disclosure of confidential information may be legally required. This discussion should occur as soon as possible in the social worker–client relationship and as needed throughout the course of the relationship.

(f) When social workers provide counseling services to families, couples, or groups, social workers should seek agreement among the parties involved concerning each individual's right to confidentiality and obligation to preserve the confidentiality of information shared by others. Social workers should inform participants in family, couples, or group counseling that social workers cannot guarantee that all participants will honor such agreements.

(g) Social workers should inform clients involved in family, couples, marital, or group counseling of the social worker's, employer's, and agency's policy concerning the social worker's disclosure of confidential information among the parties involved in the counseling.

(h) Social workers should not disclose confidential information to third-party payers unless clients have authorized such disclosure.

(i) Social workers should not discuss confidential information in any setting unless privacy can be ensured. Social workers should not discuss confidential information in public or semipublic areas such as hallways, waiting rooms, elevators, and restaurants.

(j) Social workers should protect the confidentiality of clients during legal proceedings to the extent permitted by law. When a court of law or other legally authorized body orders social workers to disclose confidential or privileged information without a client's consent and such disclosure could cause harm to the client, social workers should request that the court withdraw the order or limit the order as narrowly as possible or maintain the records under seal, unavailable for public inspection.

(k) Social workers should protect the confidentiality of clients when responding to requests from members of the media.

(l) Social workers should protect the confidentiality of clients' written and electronic records and other sensitive information. Social workers should take reasonable steps to ensure that clients' records are stored in a secure location and that clients' records are not available to others who are not authorized to have access.

(m) Social workers should take precautions to ensure and maintain the confidentiality of information transmitted to other parties through the use of computers, electronic mail, facsimile machines, telephones and telephone answering machines, and other electronic or computer technology. Disclosure of identifying information should be avoided whenever possible.

(n) Social workers should transfer or dispose of clients' records in a manner that protects clients' confidentiality and is consistent with state statutes governing records and social work licensure.

(o) Social workers should take reasonable precautions to protect client confidentiality in the event of the social worker's termination of practice, incapacitation, or death.

(p) Social workers should not disclose identifying information when discussing clients for teaching or training purposes unless the client has consented to disclosure of confidential information.

(q) Social workers should not disclose identifying information when discussing clients with consultants unless the client has consented to disclosure of confidential information or there is a compelling need for such disclosure.

(r) Social workers should protect the confidentiality of deceased clients consistent with the preceding standards.

1.08 Access to Records

(a) Social workers should provide clients with reasonable access to records concerning the clients. Social workers who are concerned that clients' access to their records could cause serious misunderstanding or harm to the client should provide assistance in interpreting the records and consultation with the client regarding the records. Social workers should limit clients' access to their records, or portions of their records, only in exceptional circumstances when there is compelling evidence that such access would cause serious harm to the client. Both clients' requests and the rationale for withholding some or all of the record should be documented in clients' files.

(b) When providing clients with access to their records, social workers should take steps to protect the confidentiality of other individuals identified or discussed in such records.

1.09 **Sexual Relationships**

(a) Social workers should under no circumstances engage in sexual activities or sexual contact with current clients, whether such contact is consensual or forced.

(b) Social workers should not engage in sexual activities or sexual contact with clients' relatives or other individuals with whom clients maintain a close personal relationship when there is a risk of exploitation or potential harm to the client. Sexual activity or sexual contact with clients' relatives or other individuals with whom clients maintain a personal relationship has the potential to be harmful to the client and may make it difficult for the social worker and client to maintain appropriate professional boundaries. Social workers—not their clients, their clients' relatives, or other individuals with whom the client maintains a personal relationship—assume the full burden for setting clear, appropriate, and culturally sensitive boundaries.

(c) Social workers should not engage in sexual activities or sexual contact with former clients because of the potential for harm to the client. If social workers engage in conduct contrary to this prohibition or claim that an exception to this prohibition is warranted because of extraordinary circumstances, it is social workers—not their clients—who assume the full burden of demonstrating that the former client has not been exploited, coerced, or manipulated, intentionally or unintentionally.

(d) Social workers should not provide clinical services to individuals with whom they have had a prior sexual relationship. Providing clinical services to a former sexual partner has the potential to be harmful to the individual and is likely to make it difficult for the social worker and individual to maintain appropriate professional boundaries.

1.10 **Physical Contact**

Social workers should not engage in physical contact with clients when there is a possibility of psychological harm to the client as a result of the contact (such as cradling or caressing clients). Social workers who engage in appropriate physical contact with clients are responsible for setting clear, appropriate, and culturally sensitive boundaries that govern such physical contact.

1.11 Sexual Harassment

Social workers should not sexually harass clients. Sexual harassment includes sexual advances, sexual solicitation, requests for sexual favors, and other verbal or physical conduct of a sexual nature.

1.12 Derogatory Language

Social workers should not use derogatory language in their written or verbal communications to or about clients. Social workers should use accurate and respectful language in all communications to and about clients.

1.13 Payment for Services

(a) When setting fees, social workers should ensure that the fees are fair, reasonable, and commensurate with the services performed. Consideration should be given to clients' ability to pay.

(b) Social workers should avoid accepting goods or services from clients as payment for professional services. Bartering arrangements, particularly involving services, create the potential for conflicts of interest, exploitation, and inappropriate boundaries in social workers' relationships with clients. Social workers should explore and may participate in bartering only in very limited circumstances when it can be demonstrated that such arrangements are an accepted practice among professionals in the local community, considered to be essential for the provision of services, negotiated without coercion, and entered into at the client's initiative and with the client's informed consent. Social workers who accept goods or services from clients as payment for professional services assume the full burden of demonstrating that this arrangement will not be detrimental to the client or the professional relationship.

(c) Social workers should not solicit a private fee or other remuneration for providing services to clients who are entitled to such available services through the social workers' employer or agency.

1.14 Clients Who Lack Decision-Making Capacity

When social workers act on behalf of clients who lack the capacity to make informed decisions, social workers should take reasonable steps to safeguard the interests and rights of those clients.

1.15 **Interruption of Services**

Social workers should make reasonable efforts to ensure continuity of services in the event that services are interrupted by factors such as unavailability, relocation, illness, disability, or death.

1.16 **Termination of Services**

(a) Social workers should terminate services to clients and professional relationships with them when such services and relationships are no longer required or no longer serve the clients' needs or interests.

(b) Social workers should take reasonable steps to avoid abandoning clients who are still in need of services. Social workers should withdraw services precipitously only under unusual circumstances, giving careful consideration to all factors in the situation and taking care to minimize possible adverse effects. Social workers should assist in making appropriate arrangements for continuation of services when necessary.

(c) Social workers in fee-for-service settings may terminate services to clients who are not paying an overdue balance if the financial contractual arrangements have been made clear to the client, if the client does not pose an imminent danger to self or others, and if the clinical and other consequences of the current nonpayment have been addressed and discussed with the client.

(d) Social workers should not terminate services to pursue a social, financial, or sexual relationship with a client.

(e) Social workers who anticipate the termination or interruption of services to clients should notify clients promptly and seek the transfer, referral, or continuation of services in relation to the clients' needs and preferences.

(f) Social workers who are leaving an employment setting should inform clients of appropriate options for the continuation of services and of the benefits and risks of the options.

2. **Social Workers' Ethical Responsibilities to Colleagues**

2.01 **Respect**

(a) Social workers should treat colleagues with respect and should represent accurately and fairly the qualifications, views, and obligations of colleagues.

(b) Social workers should avoid unwarranted negative criticism of colleagues in communications with clients or with other professionals. Unwarranted negative criticism may include demeaning comments that refer to colleagues' level of competence or to individuals attributes such as race, ethnicity, national origin, color, sex, sexual orientation, age, marital status, political belief, religion, and mental or physical disability.

(c) Social workers should cooperate with social work colleagues and with colleagues of other professions when such cooperation serves the well-being of clients.

2.02 Confidentiality

Social workers should respect confidential information shared by colleagues in the course of their professional relationships and transactions. Social workers should ensure that such colleagues understand social workers' obligation to respect confidentiality and any exceptions related to it.

2.03 Interdisciplinary Collaboration

(a) Social workers who are members of an interdisciplinary team should participate in and contribute to decisions that affect the well-being of clients by drawing on the perspectives, values, and experiences of the social work profession. Professional and ethical obligations of the interdisciplinary team as a whole and of its individual members should be clearly established.

(b) Social workers for whom a team decision raises ethical concerns should attempt to resolve the disagreement through appropriate channels. If the disagreement cannot be resolved, social workers should pursue other avenues to address their concerns consistent with client well-being.

2.04 Disputes Involving Colleagues

(a) Social workers should not take advantage of a dispute between a colleague and an employer to obtain a position or otherwise advance the social workers' own interests.

(b) Social workers should not exploit clients in disputes with colleagues or engage clients in any inappropriate discussion of conflicts between social workers and their colleagues.

2.05 Consultation

(a) Social workers should seek the advice and counsel of colleagues whenever such consultation is in the best interests of clients.

(b) Social workers should keep themselves informed about colleagues' areas of expertise and competencies. Social workers should seek consultation only from colleagues who have demonstrated knowledge, expertise, and competence related to the subject of the consultation.

(c) When consulting with colleagues about clients, social workers should disclose the least amount of information necessary to achieve the purposes of the consultation.

2.06 Referral for Services

(a) Social workers should refer clients to other professionals when the other professionals' specialized knowledge or expertise is needed to serve clients fully or when social workers believe that they are not being effective or making reasonable progress with clients and that additional service is required.

(b) Social workers who refer clients to other professionals should take appropriate steps to facilitate an orderly transfer of responsibility. Social workers who refer clients to other professionals should disclose, with clients' consent, all pertinent information to the new service providers.

(c) Social workers are prohibited from giving or receiving payment for a referral when no professional service is provided by the referring social worker.

2.07 Sexual Relationships

(a) Social workers who function as supervisors or educators should not engage in sexual activities or contact with supervisees, students, trainees, or other colleagues over whom they exercise professional authority.

(b) Social workers should avoid engaging in sexual relationships with colleagues when there is potential for a conflict of interest. Social workers who become involved in, or anticipate becoming involved in, a sexual relationship with a colleague have a duty to transfer professional responsibilities, when necessary, to avoid a conflict of interest.

2.08 Sexual Harassment

Social workers should not sexually harass supervisees, students, trainees, or colleagues. Sexual harassment includes sexual advances, sexual solicitation, requests for sexual favors, and other verbal or physical conduct of a sexual nature.

2.09 Impairment of Colleagues

(a) Social workers who have direct knowledge of a social work colleague's impairment that is due to personal problems, psychosocial distress, substance abuse, or mental health difficulties and that interferes with practice effectiveness should consult with that colleague when feasible and assist the colleague in taking remedial action.

(b) Social workers who believe that a social work colleague's impairment interferes with practice effectiveness and that the colleague has not taken adequate steps to address the impairment should take action through appropriate channels established by employers, agencies, NASW, licensing and regulatory bodies, and other professional organizations.

2.10 Incompetence of Colleagues

(a) Social workers who have direct knowledge of a social work colleague's incompetence should consult with that colleague when feasible and assist the colleague in taking remedial action.

(b) Social workers who believe that a social work colleague is incompetent and has not taken adequate steps to address the incompetence should take action through appropriate channels established by employers, agencies, NASW, licensing and regulatory bodies, and other professional organizations.

2.11 Unethical Conduct of Colleagues

(a) Social workers should take adequate measures to discourage, prevent, expose, and correct the unethical conduct of colleagues.

(b) Social workers should be knowledgeable about established policies and procedures for handling concerns about colleagues' unethical behavior. Social workers should be familiar with national, state, and local procedures for handling ethics complaints. These include policies and procedures created by NASW, licensing and regulatory bodies, employers, agencies, and other professional organizations.

(c) Social workers who believe that a colleague has acted unethically should seek resolution by discussing their concerns with the colleague when feasible and when such discussion is likely to be productive.

(d) When necessary, social workers who believe that a colleague has acted unethically should take action through appropriate formal channels (such as contacting a state licensing board or regulatory body, an NASW committee on inquiry, or other professional ethics committees).

(e) Social workers should defend and assist colleagues who are unjustly charged with unethical conduct.

3. **Social Workers' Ethical Responsibilities in Practice Settings**
   3.01 **Supervision and Consultation**
   (a) Social workers who provide supervision or consultation should have the necessary knowledge and skill to supervise or consult appropriately and should do so only within their areas of knowledge and competence.
   (b) Social workers who provide supervision or consultation are responsible for setting clear, appropriate, and culturally sensitive boundaries.
   (c) Social workers should not engage in any dual or multiple relationships with supervisees in which there is a risk of exploitation of or potential harm to the supervisee.
   (d) Social workers who provide supervision should evaluate supervisees' performance in a manner that is fair and respectful.
   3.02 **Education and Training**
   (a) Social workers who function as educators, field instructors for students, or trainers should provide instruction only within their areas of knowledge and competence and should provide instruction based on the most current information and knowledge available in the profession.
   (b) Social workers who function as educators or field instructors for students should evaluate students' performance in a manner that is fair and respectful.
   (c) Social workers who function as educators or field instructors for students should take reasonable steps to ensure that clients are routinely informed when services are being provided by students.
   (d) Social workers who function as educators or field instructors for students should not engage in any dual or multiple relationships with students in which there is a risk of exploitation or potential harm to the student. Social work educators and field instructors are responsible for setting clear, appropriate, and culturally sensitive boundaries.
   3.03 **Performance Evaluation**
   Social workers who have responsibility for evaluating the performance of others should fulfill such responsibility in a fair and considerate manner and on the basis of clearly stated criteria.

3.04 Client Records

(a) Social workers should take reasonable steps to ensure that documentation in records is accurate and reflects the services provided.

(b) Social workers should include sufficient and timely documentation in records to facilitate the delivery of services and to ensure continuity of services provided to clients in the future.

(c) Social workers' documentation should protect clients' privacy to the extent that is possible and appropriate and should include only information that is directly relevant to the delivery of services.

(d) Social workers should store records following the termination of services to ensure reasonable future access. Records should be maintained for the number of years required by state statutes or relevant contracts.

3.05 Billing

Social workers should establish and maintain billing practices that accurately reflect the nature and extent of services provided and that identify who provided the service in the practice setting.

3.06 Client Transfer

(a) When an individual who is receiving services from another agency or colleague contacts a social worker for services, the social worker should carefully consider the client's needs before agreeing to provide services. To minimize possible confusion and conflict, social workers should discuss with potential clients the nature of the clients' current relationship with other service providers and the implications, including possible benefits or risks, of entering into a relationship with a new service provider.

(b) If a new client has been served by another agency or colleague, social workers should discuss with the client whether consultation with the previous service provider is in the client's best interest.

3.07 Administration

(a) Social work administrators should advocate within and outside their agencies for adequate resources to meet clients' needs.

(b) Social workers should advocate for resource allocation procedures that are open and fair. When not all clients' needs can be met, an allocation procedure should be developed that is nondiscriminatory and based on appropriate and consistently applied principles.

(c) Social workers who are administrators should take reasonable steps to ensure that adequate agency or organizational resources are available to provide appropriate staff supervision.

(d) Social work administrators should take reasonable steps to ensure that the working environment for which they are responsible is consistent with and encourages compliance with the *NASW Code of Ethics*. Social work administrators should take reasonable steps to eliminate any conditions in their organizations that violate, interfere with, or discourage compliance with the *Code*.

3.08 Continuing Education and Staff Development

Social work administrators and supervisors should take reasonable steps to provide or arrange for continuing education and staff development for all staff for whom they are responsible. Continuing education and staff development should address current knowledge and emerging developments related to social work practice and ethics.

3.09 Commitments to Employers

(a) Social workers generally should adhere to commitments made to employers and employing organizations.

(b) Social workers should work to improve employing agencies' policies and procedures and the efficiency and effectiveness of their services.

(c) Social workers should take reasonable steps to ensure that employers are aware of social workers' ethical obligations as set forth in the *NASW Code of Ethics* and of the implications of those obligations for social work practice.

(d) Social workers should not allow an employing organization's policies, procedures, regulations, or administrative orders to interfere with their ethical practice of social work. Social workers should take reasonable steps to ensure that their employing organizations' practices are consistent with the *NASW Code of Ethics*.

(e) Social workers should act to prevent and eliminate discrimination in the employing organization's work assignments and in its employment policies and practices.

(f) Social workers should accept employment or arrange student field placements only in organizations that exercise fair personnel practices.

(g) Social workers should be diligent stewards of the resources of their employing organizations, wisely conserving funds where appropriate and never misappropriating funds or using them for unintended purposes.

3.10 Labor–Management Disputes

(a) Social workers may engage in organized action, including the formation of and participation in labor unions, to improve services to clients and working conditions.

(b) The actions of social workers who are involved in labor–management disputes, job actions, or labor strikes should be guided by the profession's values, ethical principles, and ethical standards. Reasonable differences of opinion exist among social workers concerning their primary obligation as professionals during an actual or threatened labor strike or job action. Social workers should carefully examine relevant issues and their possible impact on clients before deciding on a course of action.

4. Social Workers' Ethical Responsibilities as Professionals

4.01 Competence

(a) Social workers should accept responsibility or employment only on the basis of existing competence or the intention to acquire the necessary competence.

(b) Social workers should strive to become and remain proficient in professional practice and the performance of professional functions. Social workers should critically examine and keep current with emerging knowledge relevant to social work. Social workers should routinely review the professional literature and participate in continuing education relevant to social work practice and social work ethics.

(c) Social workers should base practice on recognized knowledge, including empirically based knowledge, relevant to social work and social work ethics.

4.02 Discrimination

Social workers should not practice, condone, facilitate, or collaborate with any form of discrimination on the basis of race, ethnicity, national origin, color, sex, sexual orientation, age, marital status, political belief, religion, or mental or physical disability.

4.03 Private Conduct

Social workers should not permit their private conduct to interfere with their ability to fulfill their professional responsibilities.

4.04 Dishonesty, Fraud, and Deception
Social workers should not participate in, condone, or be associated with dishonesty, fraud, or deception.

4.05 Impairment
(a) Social workers should not allow their own personal problems, psychosocial distress, legal problems, substance abuse, or mental health difficulties to interfere with their professional judgment and performance or to jeopardize the best interests of people for whom they have a professional responsibility.

(b) Social workers whose personal problems, psychosocial distress, legal problems, substance abuse, or mental health difficulties interfere with their professional judgment and performance should immediately seek consultation and take appropriate remedial action by seeking professional help, making adjustments in workload, terminating practice, or taking any other steps necessary to protect clients and others.

4.06 Misrepresentation
(a) Social workers should make clear distinctions between statements made and actions engaged in as a private individual and as a representative of the social work profession, a professional social work organization, or the social worker's employing agency.

(b) Social workers who speak on behalf of professional social work organizations should accurately represent the official and authorized positions of the organizations.

(c) Social workers should ensure that their representations to clients, agencies, and the public of professional qualifications, credentials, education, competence, affiliations, services provided, or results to be achieved are accurate. Social workers should claim only those relevant professional credentials they actually possess and take steps to correct any inaccuracies or misrepresentations of their credentials by others.

4.07 Solicitations
(a) Social workers should not engage in uninvited solicitation of potential clients who, because of their circumstances, are vulnerable to undue influence, manipulation, or coercion.

(b) Social workers should not engage in solicitation of testimonial endorsements (including solicitation of consent to use a client's prior statement as a testimonial endorsement) from current clients or from other people who, because of their particular circumstances, are vulnerable to undue influence.

4.08 Acknowledging Credit

(a) Social workers should take responsibility and credit, including authorship credit, only for work they have actually performed and to which they have contributed.

(b) Social workers should honestly acknowledge the work of and the contributions made by others.

5. Social Workers' Ethical Responsibilities to the Social Work Profession

5.01 Integrity of the Profession

(a) Social workers should work toward the maintenance and promotion of high standards of practice.

(b) Social workers should uphold and advance the values, ethics, knowledge, and mission of the profession. Social workers should protect, enhance, and improve the integrity of the profession through appropriate study and research, active discussion, and responsible criticism of the profession.

(c) Social workers should contribute time and professional expertise to activities that promote respect for the value, integrity, and competence of the social work profession. These activities may include teaching, research, consultation, service, legislative testimony, presentations in the community, and participation in their professional organizations.

(d) Social workers should contribute to the knowledge base of social work and share with colleagues their knowledge related to practice, research, and ethics. Social workers should seek to contribute to the profession's literature and to share their knowledge at professional meetings and conferences.

(e) Social workers should act to prevent the unauthorized and unqualified practice of social work.

5.02 Evaluation and Research

(a) Social workers should monitor and evaluate policies, the implementation of programs, and practice interventions.

(b) Social workers should promote and facilitate evaluation and research to contribute to the development of knowledge.

(c) Social workers should critically examine and keep current with emerging knowledge relevant to social work and fully use evaluation and research evidence in their professional practice.

(d) Social workers engaged in evaluation or research should carefully consider possible consequences and should follow guidelines developed for the protection of evaluation and research participants. Appropriate institutional review boards should be consulted.

(e) Social workers engaged in evaluation or research should obtain voluntary and written informed consent from participants, when appropriate, without any implied or actual deprivation or penalty for refusal to participate; without undue inducement to participate; and with due regard for participants' well-being, privacy, and dignity. Informed consent should include information about the nature, extent, and duration of the participation requested and disclosure of the risks and benefits of participation in the research.

(f) When evaluation or research participants are incapable of giving informed consent, social workers should provide an appropriate explanation to the participants, obtain the participants' assent to the extent they are able, and obtain written consent from an appropriate proxy.

(g) Social workers should never design or conduct evaluation or research that does not use consent procedures, such as certain forms of naturalistic observation and archival research, unless rigorous and responsible review of the research has found it to be justified because of its prospective scientific, educational, or applied value and unless equally effective alternative procedures that do not involve waiver of consent are not feasible.

(h) Social workers should inform participants of their right to withdraw from evaluation and research at any time without penalty.

(i) Social workers should take appropriate steps to ensure that participants in evaluation and research have access to appropriate supportive services.

(j) Social workers engaged in evaluation or research should protect participants from unwarranted physical or mental distress, harm, danger, or deprivation.

(k) Social workers engaged in the evaluation of services should discuss collected information only for professional purposes and only with people professionally concerned with this information.

(l) Social workers engaged in evaluation or research should ensure the anonymity or confidentiality of participants and of the data obtained from them. Social workers should inform participants of any limits of confidentiality, the measures that will be taken to ensure confidentiality, and when any records containing research data will be destroyed.

(m) Social workers who report evaluation and research results should protect participants' confidentiality by omitting identifying information unless proper consent has been obtained authorizing disclosure.

(n) Social workers should report evaluation and research findings accurately. They should not fabricate or falsify results and should take steps to correct any errors later found in published data using standard publication methods.

(o) Social workers engaged in evaluation or research should be alert to and avoid conflicts of interest and dual relationships with participants, should inform participants when a real or potential conflict of interest arises, and should take steps to resolve the issue in a manner that makes participants' interests primary.

(p) Social workers should educate themselves, their students, and their colleagues about responsible research practices.

6. **Social Workers' Ethical Responsibilities to the Broader Society**

   6.01 **Social Welfare**

   Social workers should promote the general welfare of society, from local to global levels, and the development of people, their communities, and their environments. Social workers should advocate for living conditions conducive to the fulfillment of basic human needs and should promote social, economic, political, and cultural values and institutions that are compatible with the realization of social justice.

   6.02 **Public Participation**

   Social workers should facilitate informed participation by the public in shaping social policies and institutions.

   6.03 **Public Emergencies**

   Social workers should provide appropriate professional services in public emergencies to the greatest extent possible.

   6.04 **Social and Political Action**

   (a) Social workers should engage in social and political action that seeks to ensure that all people have equal access to the resources, employment, services, and opportunities they require to meet their basic human needs and to develop fully. Social workers should be aware of the impact of the political arena on practice and should advocate for changes in policy and legislation to improve social conditions in order to meet basic human needs and promote social justice.

(b) Social workers should act to expand choice and opportunity for all people, with special regard for vulnerable, disadvantaged, oppressed, and exploited people and groups.

(c) Social workers should promote conditions that encourage respect for cultural and social diversity within the United States and globally. Social workers should promote policies and practices that demonstrate respect for difference, support the expansion of cultural knowledge and resources, advocate for programs and institutions that demonstrate cultural competence, and promote policies that safeguard the rights of and confirm equity and social justice for all people.

(d) Social workers should act to prevent and eliminate domination of, exploitation of, and discrimination against any person, group, or class on the basis of race, ethnicity, national origin, color, sex, sexual orientation, age, marital status, political belief, religion, or mental or physical disability.

Relevant Literature

Administration and Organizational Ethics

Cooper, T. (2006). *The responsible administrator: An approach to ethics for the administrative role* (5th ed.). San Francisco: Jossey-Bass.

Joseph, M. (1983). The ethics of organizations: Shifting values and ethical dilemmas. *Administration in Social Work, 7,* 47–57.

Levy, C. (1982). *Guide to ethical decisions and actions for social service administrators.* New York: Haworth Press.

Menzel, D. (2006). *Ethics management for public administrators: Building organizations of integrity.* Armonk, NY: M. E. Sharpe.

Reamer, F. G. (1993). Liability issues in social work administration. *Administration in Social Work, 17,* 11–25.

Reamer, F. G. (2000). Administrative ethics. In R. J. Patti (Ed.), *The handbook of social welfare management* (pp. 69–85). Thousand Oaks, CA: Sage Publications.

Reamer, F. G. (2007). Challenging unethical agency policies [Eye on Ethics]. *Social Work Today, 7,* 62–63.

Reamer, F. G. (2008). Administrative challenges [Eye on Ethics]. *Social Work Today, 8,* 8–9.

Boundary Issues and Dual Relationships

Gutheil, T., & Gabbard, G. (1993). The concept of boundaries in clinical practice. Theoretical and risk management dimensions. *American Journal of Psychiatry, 150,* 188–196.

Herlihy, B., & Corey, B. (2006). *Boundary issues in counseling: Multiple roles and responsibilities.* Alexandria, VA: American Counseling Association.

Kagle, J., & Giebelhausen, P. (1994). Dual relationships and professional boundaries. *Social Work, 39,* 213–220.

Peterson, M. (1992). *At personal risk: Boundary violations in professional-client relationships.* New York: Norton.

Reamer, F. G. (2001). *Tangled relationships: Managing boundary issues in the human services.* New York: Columbia University Press.

Reamer, F. G. (2002). Eye on ethics: Managing boundaries and dual relationships [Eye on Ethics]. *Social Work Today, 2,* 22–23.

Reamer, F. G. (2003). Boundary issues in social work: Managing dual relationships. *Social Work, 48,* 121–133.

Strom-Gottfried, K. (1999). Professional boundaries: An analysis of violations by social workers. *Families in Society, 80,* 439–449.

Syme, G. (2003). *Dual relationships in counseling and psychotherapy.* London: Sage Publications.

Zur, O. (2007). *Boundaries in psychotherapy: Ethical and clinical explorations.* Washington, DC: American Psychological Association.

Codes of Ethics

Brandl, P., & Maguire, M. (2001). Codes of ethics: A primer on their purpose, development, and use. *Journal for Quality and Participation, 25,* 8–12.

Freeman, S., Engels, D., & Altekruse, M. (2004). Foundations for ethical standards and codes: The role of moral philosophy and theory in ethics. *Counseling and Values, 48,* 163–173.

Freud, S., & Krug, S. (2002). Beyond the Code of Ethics, Part I: Complexities of ethical decision making in social work practice. *Families in Society, 83,* 474–482.

Freud, S., & Krug, S. (2002). Beyond the Code of Ethics, Part II: Dual relationships revisited. *Families in Society, 83,* 483–492.

Jamal, K., & Bowie, N. (1995). Theoretical considerations for a meaningful code of professional ethics. *Journal of Business Ethics, 14,* 703–714.

Levy, C. (1974). On the development of a code of ethics. *Social Work, 19,* 207–216.

Montgomery, V. (2003). Codes of ethics as living documents. *Public Integrity, 5,* 331–346.

National Association of Social Workers. (2000). *Code of ethics of the National Association of Social Workers.* Washington, DC: Author.

National Association of Social Workers, Code of Ethics Revision Committee. (1998). *Current controversies in social work ethics: Case examples.* Washington, DC: Author.

Reamer, F. G. (1997). Ethical standards in social work: The NASW code of ethics. In R. Edwards (Ed.-in-Chief), *Encyclopedia of social work* (19th ed. Suppl., pp. 113–123). Washington, DC: NASW Press.

Reamer, F. G. (2006). *Ethical standards in social work: A review of the NASW code of ethics* (2nd ed.). Washington, DC: NASW Press.

Reamer, F. G. (2008). Ethical standards in social work: The NASW code of ethics. In T. Mizrahi & L. Davis (Eds.-in-Chief), *Encyclopedia of social work* (20th ed., pp. 391–397). New York and Washington, DC: Oxford University Press and NASW Press.

Confidentiality and Privileged Communication

Alexander, R., Jr. (1997). Social workers and privileged communication in the federal legal system. *Social Work, 42,* 387–391.

Arnold, S. (1970). Confidential communication and the social worker. *Social Work, 15,* 61–67.

Dickson, D. T. (1998). *Confidentiality and privacy in social work.* New York: Free Press.

Gelman, S., Pollack, D., & Weiner, A. (1999). Confidentiality of social work records in the computer age. *Social Work, 44,* 243–252.

Kopels, S., & Kagle, J. (1993). Do social workers have a duty to warn? *Social Service Review, 67,* 101–126.

Reamer, F. G. (1991). AIDS, social work, and the "duty to protect." *Social Work, 36,* 56–60.

Reamer, F. G. (2001). Managing client confidentiality: Lessons in practical ethics. *Social Work Today, 1,* 18–21.

Reamer, F. G. (2005). Update on confidentiality issues in practice with children: Ethics risk management [Trends & Issues]. *Children & Schools, 27,* 117–120.

Reynolds, M. (1976). Threats to confidentiality. *Social Work, 21,* 108–113.

Rock, B., & Congress, E. (1999). The new confidentiality for the 21st century in a managed care environment. *Social Work, 44,* 253–262.

VandeCreek, L., Knapp, S., & Herzog, C. (1988). Privileged communication for social workers. *Social Casework, 69,* 28–34.

Weil, M., & Sanchez, E. (1983). The impact of the *Tarasoff* decision on clinical social work practice. *Social Service Review, 57,* 112–124.

Core Concepts and Principles

Abramson, M. (1996). Reflections on knowing oneself ethically: Toward a framework for social work practice. *Families in Society, 77,* 195–201.

Beauchamp, T., & Childress, J. (2008). *Principles of biomedical ethics* (6th ed.). New York: Oxford University Press.

Bernstein, B., & Hartsell, T. (2008). *The portable ethicist for mental health professionals* (2nd ed.). New York: John Wiley & Sons.

Bershoff, D. (Ed.). (2003). *Ethical conflicts in psychology* (3rd ed.). Washington, DC: American Psychological Association.

Cahn, S., & Markie, P. (2008). *Ethics: History, theory, and contemporary issues* (4th ed.). New York: Oxford University Press.

Congress, E. (2000). *Social work values and ethics.* Chicago: Nelson-Hall.

Corey, G., Corey, M., & Callanan, P. (2006). *Issues and ethics in the helping professions* (7th ed.). Pacific Grove, CA.: Brooks/Cole.

Curtler, H. (2004). *Ethical argument: Critical thinking in ethics* (2nd ed.). New York: Oxford University Press.

Dean, R., & Rhodes, M. (1992). Ethical-clinical tensions in clinical practice. *Social Work, 39,* 128–132.

Dolgoff, R., Loewenberg, F., & Harrington, D. (2008). *Ethical decisions for social work practice* (8th ed.). Belmont, CA: Brooks Cole.

Emmet, D. (1962). Ethics and the social worker. *British Journal of Psychiatric Social Work, 6,* 165–172.

Frankena, W. (1988). *Ethics* (2nd ed.). Englewood Cliffs, NJ: Prentice-Hall.

Gambrill, E., & Pruger, R. (Eds.). (1997). *Controversial issues in social work: Ethics, values, and obligations.* Boston: Allyn & Bacon.

Goldstein, H. (1987). The neglected moral link in social work practice. *Social Work, 32,* 181–186.

Jayaratne, S., Croxton, T., & Mattison, D. (1997). Social work professional standards: An exploratory study. *Social Work, 42,* 187–199.

Joseph, M. (1989). Social work ethics: Historical and contemporary perspectives. *Social Thought, 15,* 4–17.

Koocher, G., & Keith-Spiegel, P. (2007). *Ethics in psychology and the mental health professions* (3rd ed.). New York: Oxford University Press.

Levy, C. (1972). The context of social work ethics. *Social Work, 17,* 488–493.

Levy, C. (1973). The value base of social work. *Journal of Education for Social Work, 9,* 34–42.

Levy C. (1976). *Social work ethics.* New York: Human Sciences Press.

Linzer, N. (1999). *Resolving ethical dilemmas in social work practice.* Boston: Allyn & Bacon.

Manning, S. (1997). The social worker as moral citizen: Ethics in action. *Social Work, 42,* 223–230.

Mattison, M. (2000). Ethical decision making: The person in the process. *Social Work, 45,* 201–212.

Plant, R. (1970). *Social and moral theory in casework.* London: Routledge and Kegan Paul.

Reamer, F. G. (1979). Fundamental ethical issues in social work: An essay review. *Social Service Review, 53,* 229–243.

Reamer, F. G. (1980). Ethical content in social work. *Social Casework, 61,* 531–540.

Reamer, F. G. (1982). Conflicts of professional duty in social work. *Social Casework, 63,* 579–585.

Reamer, F. G. (1983). Ethical dilemmas in social work practice. *Social Work, 28,* 31–35.

Reamer, F. G. (1985). The emergence of bioethics in social work. *Health & Social Work, 10,* 271–281.

Reamer, F. G. (1986). The use of modern technology in social work: Ethical dilemmas [Comments on Currents]. *Social Work, 31,* 469–472.

Reamer, F. G. (1987). Social work: Calling or career? *Hastings Center Report* (Suppl.), *17,* 14–15.

Reamer, F. G. (1987). Values and ethics. In A. Minahan (Ed.-in-Chief), *Encyclopedia of social work* (18th ed., Vol. 2, pp. 801–809). Silver Spring, MD: National Association of Social Workers.

Reamer, F. G. (1989). Toward ethical practice: The relevance of ethical theory. *Social Thought, 15,* 67–78.

Reamer, F. G. (1990). *Ethical dilemmas in social service* (2nd ed.). New York: Columbia University Press.

Reamer, F. G. (1992). Social work and the public good: Calling or career? In P. N. Reid & P. Popple (Eds.), *The moral purposes of social work: The character and intentions of a profession* (pp. 11–33). Chicago: Nelson-Hall.

Reamer, F. G. (1993). AIDS and social work: The ethics and civil liberties agenda. *Social Work, 38,* 412–419.

Reamer, F. G. (1994). Social work values and ethics. In F. G. Reamer (Ed.), *The foundations of social work knowledge* (pp. 195–230). New York: Columbia University Press.

Reamer, F. G. (1995). Ethics and values. In R. L. Edwards (Ed.-in-Chief), *Encyclopedia of social work* (19th ed., pp. 893–902). Washington, DC: NASW Press.

Reamer, F. G. (1997). Ethical issues for social work practice. In M. Reisch & E. Gambrill (Eds.), *Social work in the 21st century* (pp. 340–349). Thousand Oaks, CA: Pine Forge Forge Press.

Reamer, F. G. (1998). The evolution of social work ethics. *Social Work, 43,* 488–500.

Reamer, F. G. (1998). Social work. In R. Chadwick (Ed-in-Chief), *Encyclopedia of applied ethics* (Vol. 4, pp. 169–180). San Diego: Academic Press.

Reamer, F. G. (2000). Ethical issues in direct practice. In P. Allen-Meares & C. Garvin (Eds.), *The handbook of social work direct practice* (pp. 589–610). Thousand Oaks, CA: Sage Publications.

Reamer, F. G. (2001). Ethical issues. In B. A. Thyer (Ed.), *The handbook of social work research methods* (pp. 429–444). Thousand Oaks, CA: Sage Publications.

Reamer, F. G. (2001). Ethics and values in clinical and community social work practice. In H. E. Briggs & K. Corcoran (Eds.), *Social work practice: Treating common clinical problems* (pp. 85–106). Chicago: Lyceum Books.

Reamer, F. G. (2002). Ethical issues in social work. In A. R. Roberts & G. J. Greene (Eds.), *Social workers' desk reference* (pp. 65–69). New York: Oxford University Press.

Reamer, F. G. (2005). Ethical and legal standards in social work: Consistency and conflict. *Families in Society, 86,* 163–169.

Reamer, F. G. (2005). Social work values and ethics: Reflections on the profession's odyssey. *Advances in Social Work, 6,* 24–32.

Reamer, F. G. (2006). *Social work values and ethics* (3rd ed.). New York: Columbia University Press.

Reamer, F. G. (2008). Ethics and values. In T. Mizrahi & L. Davis (Eds.-in-Chief), *Encyclopedia of social work* (20th ed., Vol. 2, pp. 143–151). New York and Washington, DC: Oxford University Press and NASW Press.

Reid, P., & Popple, P. (Eds.). (1992). *The moral purposes of social work.* Chicago: Nelson-Hall.

Rhodes, M. (1986). *Ethical dilemmas in social work practice.* London: Routledge and Kegan Paul.

Siporin, M. (1989). The social work ethic. *Social Thought, 15,* 42–52.

Spano, R., & Koenig, T. (2007). What is sacred when personal and professional values collide? *Journal of Social Work Values and Ethics, 4.* Retrieved August 12, 2008, from *Journal of Social Work Values and Ethics:* http://www.socialworker.com/jswve/content/view/69/54/

Strom-Gottfried, K. (2007). *Straight talk about professional ethics.* Chicago: Lyceum.

Timms, N. (1983). *Social work values: An enquiry.* London: Routledge and Kegan Paul.

Williams, B. (1993). *Morality: An introduction to ethics.* Cambridge: Cambridge University Press.

Documentation and Case Recording

Kagle, J. (1995). *Social work records* (2nd ed.). Long Grove, IL: Waveland Press.

Luepker, E., & Norton, L. (2002). *Record keeping in psychotherapy and counseling.* New York: Brunner-Routledge.

Moline, M., Williams, F., & Austin, K. (1998). *Documenting psychotherapy: Essentials for mental health professionals.* Beverly Hills, CA: Sage Publications.

Reamer, F. G. (2005). Documentation in social work: Evolving ethical and risk-management standards. *Social Work, 50,* 325–334.

Wiger, D. (2005). *The clinical documentation sourcebook: The complete paperwork resource for your mental health practice* (3rd ed.). Hoboken, NJ: John Wiley & Sons.

Ethics Committees and Ethics Consultation

Aulisio, M. (2001). Doing ethics consultation. *American Journal of Bioethics, 1,* 54–55.

Aulisio, M., Arnold, R., & Youngner, S. (2003). *Ethics consultation: From theory to practice.* Baltimore: Johns Hopkins University Press.

Cohen, C. (1988). Ethics committees. *Hastings Center Report, 18,* 11.

Conrad, A. (1989). Developing an ethics review process in a social service agency. *Social Thought, 15,* 102–115.

Cranford, R., & Doudera, E. (Eds.). (1984). *Institutional ethics committees and health care decision making.* Ann Arbor, MI: Health Administration Press.

Fletcher, J., Quist, N., & Jonsen, A. (1989). *Ethics consultation in health care.* Ann Arbor, MI: Health Administration Press.

La Puma, J. (1994). *Ethics consultation: A practical guide.* Sudbury, MA: Jones & Bartlett.

Post, L., Blustein, J., & Dubler, N. (2006). *Handbook for health care ethics committees.* Baltimore: Johns Hopkins University Press.

Reamer, F. G. (1987). Ethics committees in social work. *Social Work, 32,* 188–192.

Reamer, F. G. (1995). Ethics consultation in social work. *Social Thought, 18,* 3–16.

Reamer, F. G. (2005). The emergence of agency ethics committees in social work [Eye on Ethics]. *Social Work Today, 5,* 58–59.

Reamer, F. G. (2007). Eye on ethics: The importance of ethics consultation [Eye on Ethics]. *Social Work Today, 7,* 6–8.

Ethics Education

Callahan, D., & Bok, S. (Eds.). (1980). *Ethics teaching in higher education.* New York: Plenum Press.

Goldstein, H. (1998). Education for ethical dilemmas in social work practice. *Families in Society, 79,* 241–253.

Johnson, A. (1955). Educating professional social workers for ethical practice. *Social Service Review, 29,* 125–136.

Joseph, M., & Conrad, A. (1983). Teaching social work ethics for contemporary practice: An effectiveness evaluation. *Journal of Education for Social Work, 19,* 59–68.

Pumphrey, M. (1959). *The teaching of values and ethics in social work.* New York: Council on Social Work Education.

Reamer, F. G. (2001). *Ethics education in social work.* Alexandria, VA: Council on Social Work Education.

Reamer, F. G. (2001). Ethics education: New times, new challenges. *Social Work Today, 1,* 6–7.

Reamer, F. G. (2001–2002). Educating social workers about ethics: A comprehensive approach. *The Social Work Forum, 35,* 5–27.

Reamer, F. G. (2006). Revisioning ethics education in social work [Eye on Ethics]. *Social Work Today, 6,* 15–16.

Reamer, F. G., & Abramson, M. (1982). *The teaching of social work ethics.* Hastings-on-Hudson, NY: The Hastings Center.

Ethics and Managed Care

Reamer, F. G. (1997). Managing ethics under managed care. *Families in Society, 78,* 96–101.

Reamer, F. G. (1998). Managed care: Ethical considerations. In G. Schamess & A. Lightburn (Eds.), *Humane managed care?* (pp. 293–298). Washington, DC: NASW Press.

Reamer, F. G. (2001). Ethics and managed care policy. In N. W. Veeder & W. Pee-bles-Wilkins (Eds.), *Managed care services: Policy, programs, and research* (pp. 74–96). New York: Oxford University Press.

Strom-Gottfried, K. (1998). Is "ethical managed care" an oxymoron? *Families in Society, 79*, 297–307.

Ethics Risk Management

Austin, K., Moline, M., & Williams, G. (1990). *Confronting malpractice: Legal and ethical dilemmas in psychotherapy.* Newbury Park, CA: Sage Publications.

Barker, R., & Branson, D. (2000). *Forensic social work* (2nd ed.). Binghamton, NY: Haworth.

Berliner, A. (1989). Misconduct in social work practice. *Social Work, 34,* 69–72.

Bernstein, B. (1981). Malpractice: Future shock of the 1980's. *Social Casework, 62,* 175–181.

Bernstein, B., & Hartsell, T. (1998). *The portable lawyer for mental health profession-als.* New York: John Wiley & Sons.

Besharov, D. J. (1985). *The vulnerable social worker.* Silver Spring, MD: National Association of Social Workers.

Besharov, D. J., & Besharov, S. H. (1987). Teaching about liability. *Social Work, 32,* 517–522.

Bullis, R. (1995). *Clinical social worker misconduct.* Chicago: Nelson-Hall.

Houston-Vega, M., & Nuehring, E. (with Daguio, E.). (1997). *Prudent practice: A guide for managing malpractice risk.* Washington, DC: NASW Press.

Kirkpatrick, W., Reamer, F., & Sykulski, M. (2006). Social work ethics audits in health care settings: A case study. *Health & Social Work, 31,* 225–228.

McCann, C. W., & Cutler, J. P. (1979). Ethics and the alleged unethical. *Social Work, 24,* 5–8.

Madden, R. G. (1998). *Legal issues in social work, counseling, and mental health.* Thousand Oaks, CA: Sage Publications.

Reamer, F. G. (1984). Enforcing ethics in social work. *Health Matrix, 2,* 17–25.

Reamer, F. G. (1995). Malpractice claims against social workers: First facts. *Social Work, 40,* 595–601.

Reamer, F. G. (2000). The social work ethics audit: A risk-management strategy. *Social Work, 45,* 355–366.

Reamer, F. G. (2001). *The social work ethics audit: A risk-management tool.* Washington, DC: NASW Press.

Reamer, F. G. (2002). Risk management. In A. R. Roberts & G. J. Greene (Eds.), *Social workers' desk reference* (pp. 70–75). New York: Oxford University Press.

Reamer, F. G. (2003). *Social work malpractice and liability: Strategies for prevention* (2nd ed.). New York: Columbia University Press.

Reamer, F. G. (2006). Nontraditional and unorthodox interventions in social work: Ethical and legal implications. *Families in Society, 87,* 191–197.

Reamer, F. G. (2008). Social workers' management of error: Ethical and risk management issues. *Families in Society, 89,* 61–68.

Strom-Gottfried, K. (2000). Ensuring ethical practice: An examination of NASW code violations, 1986-97. *Social Work, 45,* 251–261.

Woody, R. (1997). *Legally safe mental health practice.* Madison, CT: Psychosocial Press.

Impaired Practitioners

Coombs, R. (2000). *Drug-impaired professionals.* Cambridge, MA: Harvard University Press.

Kilburg, R., Nathan, P., & Thoreson, R. (Eds.). (1986). *Professionals in distress.* Washington, DC: American Psychological Association.

Reamer, F. G. (1992). The impaired social worker. *Social Work, 37,* 165–170.

Sonnenstuhl, W. (1989). Reaching the impaired professional: Applying findings from organizational and occupational research. *Journal of Drug Issues, 19,* 533–539.

VandenBos, G., & Duthie, R. (1986). Confronting and supporting colleagues in distress. In R. R. Kilburg, P. E. Nathan, & R. W. Thoreson (Eds.), *Professionals in distress* (pp. 211–231). Washington, DC: American Psychological Association.

Research Ethics

Israel, M., & Hay, I. (2006). *Research ethics for social scientists.* Thousand Oaks, CA: Sage Publications.

Mertens, D., & Ginsberg, P. (2008). *The handbook of social research ethics.* Thousand Oaks, CA: Sage Publications.

Oliver, P. (2003). *The student's guide to research ethics.* Berkshire, England: Open University Press.

Sales, B., & Folkman, S. (2000). *Ethics in research with human participants.* Washington, DC: American Psychological Association.

Self-Determination, Paternalism, and Informed Consent

Abramson, M. (1985). The autonomy-paternalism dilemma in social work practice. *Social Casework, 66,* 387–393.

Berg, J., Appelbaum, P., Lidz, C., & Parker, L. (2001). *Informed consent: Legal theory and clinical practice* (2nd ed.). New York: Oxford University Press.

Bernstein, S. (1960). Self-determination: King or citizen in the realm of values? *Social Work, 5,* 3–8.

Biestek, F., & Gehrig, C. (1978). *Client self-determination in social work: A fifty-year history.* Chicago: Loyola University Press.

Dworkin, G. (1971). Paternalism. In R. Wasserstrom (Ed.), *Morality and the law* (pp. 107–126). Belmont, CA: Wadsworth.

Keith-Lucas, A. (1963). A critique of the principle of client self-determination. *Social Work, 8,* 66–71.

McDermott, F. E. (Ed.). (1975). *Self-determination in social work.* London: Routledge and Kegan Paul.

Perlman, H. (1965). Self-determination: Reality or illusion? *Social Service Review, 39,* 410–421.

Reamer, F. G. (1983). The concept of paternalism in social work. *Social Service Review, 57,* 254–271.

Reamer, F. G. (1983). The free will-determinism debate and social work. *Social Service Review, 57,* 626–644.

Reamer, F. G. (1987). Informed consent in social work. *Social Work, 32,* 425–429.

Reamer, F. G. (2003). The complexities of informed consent [Eye on Ethics]. *Social Work Today, 3,* 28–29.

Reamer, F. G. (2005). The challenge of paternalism in social work [Eye on Ethics]. *Social Work Today, 5,* 9–10.

Soyer, D. (1963). The right to fail. *Social Work, 8,* 72–78.

Summers, A. (1989). The meaning of informed consent in social work. *Social Thought, 15,* 128–140.

Supervision Ethics

Falvey, J. (2001). *Managing clinical supervision: Ethical practice and legal risk management.* Belmont, CA: Wadsworth.

Levy, C. (1973). The ethics of supervision. *Social Work, 18,* 14–21.

Reamer, F. G. (1989). Liability issues in social work supervision [Briefly Stated]. *Social Work, 34,* 445–448.

Index

About the Author

Frederic G. Reamer is a professor in the graduate program of the School of Social Work, Rhode Island College. His research and teaching have addressed a wide range of human service issues, including mental health, health care, criminal justice, struggling teens, and professional ethics. Dr. Reamer has served as a social worker in correctional and mental health settings and has lectured extensively nationally and internationally on the subjects of professional ethics and professional malpractice and liability. Dr. Reamer received the Presidential Award from the National Association of Social Workers and the Distinguished Contributions to Social Work Education award from the Council on Social Work Education.

Dr. Reamer's books include *Heinous Crime: Cases, Causes, and Consequences* (Columbia University Press); *Pocket Guide to Essential Human Services* (NASW Press); *Criminal Lessons: Case Studies and Commentary on Crime and Justice* (Columbia University Press); *Social Work Values and Ethics* (Columbia University Press); *Tangled Relationships: Managing Boundary Issues in the Human Services* (Columbia University Press); *Ethical Standards in Social Work: A Review of the NASW Code of Ethics* (NASW Press); *The Social Work Ethics Audit: A Risk Management Tool* (NASW Press); *Ethics Education in Social Work* (Council on Social Work Education); *The Foundations of Social Work Knowledge* (Columbia University Press; editor and contributor); *Social Work Malpractice and Liability* (Columbia University Press); *Social Work Research and Evaluation Skills* (Columbia University Press); *The Philosophical Foundations of Social Work* (Columbia University Press); *AIDS and Ethics* (Columbia University Press; editor and contributor); *Ethical Dilemmas in Social Service* (Columbia University Press); *Rehabilitating Juvenile Justice* (Columbia University Press; coauthor, Charles H. Shireman); *The Teaching of Social Work Ethics* (The Hastings Center; coauthor, Marcia Abramson); *Finding Help for Struggling Teens: A Guide for Parents and the Professionals Who Work with Them* (NASW Press; coauthor, Deborah H. Siegel); *Teens in Crisis: How the Industry Serving Struggling Teens Helps and Hurts Our Kids* (Columbia University Press; coauthor, Deborah H. Siegel).